NEW ENGLAND COASTAL

NEW ENGLAND COASTAL
HOMES THAT TELL A STORY

MARK A. HUTKER

JIM CAPPUCCINO, GREGORY EHRMAN,
THOMAS McNEILL, CHARLES E. ORR, PHIL REGAN

WRITTEN WITH KYLE HOEPNER

CONTENTS

INTRODUCTION 9

THREE GABLES 14
BREEZY POINT 36
BREACHING ROCK 54
ISLAND AERIE 78
SUNSET HILL 94
THE GRANGE 110
FEN'S EDGE 128
BIG BLUFF 146
LEDGE HOUSE 164
GREAT POND 186
HIDDEN OVERLOOK 202
BACK RIVER 222
HARBOR REACH 242

ABOUT THE FIRM 266
PROJECT CREDITS 268
ACKNOWLEDGMENTS 270

The creative work within this book represents the
evolution of Hutker Architects and its design leadership.

THE LEADERSHIP TEAM

Ryan Alcaidinho
Julie Bangert
Jim Cappuccino, AIA
Matthew Cramer, AIA
Sean Dougherty
Gregory Ehrman, AIA

Thomas McNeill, AIA
Charles e. Orr, AIA
Phil Regan
Mary Rogers
Matthew Schiffer, AIA

The firm has entrusted me with speaking for the group
in the book's introduction; their voices emerge more individually
in the narratives that accompany each project.

–Mark A. Hutker, FAIA

INTRODUCTION

"Our vision is to create a new standard for custom homes to be both passive in their demands on their environment and community, and active in their influence on the well-being of their inhabitants."

Early in my career, I was very fortunate to have the opportunity to work with writer Judy Blume, designing her family home on Martha's Vineyard. Up to that point in time, most of my professional clients had been lawyers, doctors, financiers, and the like; it was a new and welcome experience to collaborate with a fellow creative.

The project had a tough start. After the usual discussion of client needs—number of bedrooms and bathrooms, special kitchen requests, and so on—I took some time with the ideas and came back to present several design options. As Judy looked them over, it became painfully clear that we weren't on the same page (forgive me for using a literary metaphor). I was eager for this partnership to work and said, as I recall, "Judy, I feel like I'm a character in one of your books and I'm not acting the part you intended."

We walked to the Black Dog, a local waterfront restaurant, for coffee, discussing other ways to approach and execute this project. Suddenly, the conversation shifted unexpectedly. Judy began to tell me in detail about the experiences she wanted to have in her home, many of which revolved around food and hospitality. She wanted a house where friends and family could come to visit on a Friday afternoon, settle into their guest rooms, and gather around the table together as she served them dinner. Then everyone would enjoy a splendid brunch and dinner together on Saturday, and brunch again on Sunday before the guests would return to their respective homes. She envisioned each meal occurring in a different, and memorable, place on the property.

As we continued to talk, I thought, "This is so revealing and clarifying." In the stories she told about her house-to-be, she related what she dreamed might happen there rather than how big it should be, how it must look, or how the rooms must be arranged. Judy was *imagining* the home, allowing the idea of how the home would be used, rather than a specified list of design options, to convey the story of what it could be. She used a lot of "feeling" words, packed with emotion, and she essentially painted a picture of the house before we ever drew a single plan.

OPPOSITE: Celebrating the natural surroundings of a home—and making sure the architecture and materials of that home meld beautifully with its site—are always primary considerations in Hutker Architects designs like this one in the town of Aquinnah on Martha's Vineyard.

From that fateful meeting, I came to understand that what is most vital, and what needs to be examined first, is the *narrative* of each design project. Encouraging clients to tell their stories—who they are and who they want to be in their home—has been the core of the Hutker Architects approach ever since. We'll ask clients to write a series of "diary entries" describing a perfect day in their future home. What do they see themselves doing? What would bring joy and add meaning to their time? What would a rainy day be like versus a sunny day? How would they spend their weekends? How do they visualize the experience of their home changing throughout the seasons? What happens—socially and spatially—when visitors arrive, or when children bring home friends or prospective partners? These imaginative accounts help us identify the individual and collective life patterns our architecture must support: where bedrooms and kitchens and dining areas and family rooms should be located, for example, which way they ought to face, and how they need to be joined together.

ABOVE: This garage, courtyard wall, and outdoor fireplace in Greenwich, Connecticut, were constructed using stone excavated from the building site—the same type of stone that was used to build several historic structures in the town's center. Maintaining continuity with the past is an important value for Hutker Architects.

FITTING INTO PLACE

First-rate architecture is not something abstract that one can simply draw on a whim without taking into consideration the landscape in which it will live. From the beginning, the houses designed by Hutker Architects have been shaped by the marvelous diversity of New England's terrain. The region is renowned for its many miles of sandy shores, its rugged promontories, rural meadows, breathtaking ponds, woods, and mountains. The slope of a building site, its natural vegetation, the views afforded in multiple directions, and the patterns of brightness and shadow that flow and change as the sun moves throughout the day—all of these provide an essential context for design, and as architects we are unfailingly responsive to it. As we find ourselves working more and more in other regions of the United States, the same rootedness in place holds true.

A home's narrative is also influenced by a community's specific history and built environment. That's one reason our houses are rarely entirely "traditional" or entirely "modern." A residence that's mostly contemporary in overall form will still include references to local landmarks and materials or incorporate construction practices from previous centuries. A house whose facade is largely based on a vernacular model—perhaps an old farmhouse or barn—may offer a view of the scenery at its rear through a glass-and-steel window wall. Every epoch engages with the new technologies of its time, yet a firm handshake with the past ensures continuity in addition to evolution.

TOGETHER AND APART

A family home is a central site for making memories and bonding over shared experiences, but it's essential to remember that everyone, at some point, also yearns for a place where they can enjoy being solitary, sheltered, and secure. (The necessity of refuge was only amplified by the coronavirus pandemic.) That's why our houses provide a variety of areas that support gathering as well as plenty of spaces to take peaceful time away from the crowd, with easy accessibility between the two.

At the same time, "together and apart" design builds multigenerational flexibility into a residence, allowing it to be adjusted for its occupants' lives over the long term. To illustrate: perhaps we'll design a room near a couple's bedroom that can accommodate bunk beds for their kids to use while they're young, and also autonomous suites in a separate wing for the children to move into as they grow and become more independent—at which point, the bunk room can be converted into an office. Moreover, situating social and private areas in distinct zones of a home means that they can continue to offer either seclusion or fellowship as desired, even after the "little ones" return with spouses and children of their own.

PATHS AND DESTINATIONS

The act of approaching a home—first through its surrounding landscape, then entering the actual structure, and then moving through its interiors—should be a compelling, memorable journey; Hutker Architects designs always keep this experience in mind.

The routes for moving around inside and outside Hutker homes are organized as paths leading toward visual destinations. Every corridor or progression between rooms has a goal in the distance, whether it be a piece of art or a splendidly framed window view. Wayfinding supports the story of where you are, where you will soon be, and what motivates you to go there.

Transitions in our houses come in several forms. There is the main entry, which invariably gets special treatment as a space to welcome and establish the initial sense of "home." We also employ what we refer to as "hyphens"—small connectors, often glass-enclosed, that link two larger architectural volumes—and "thresholds," which are thicker and weightier than a simple door or opening between rooms. Significant passages are signposted by a change in structure, ceiling form, and height, and often by a change in materials as well. We call it "activating the space in between." The common element is *time*; you are transported somewhere else and need a moment to notice and appreciate the trip.

Destinations that attract the eye and the mind are equally crucial within a room. Particularly in what we term the "life room"—that all-important centerpiece where living, dining, cooking, and general fellowship take place—there should be more than one source of light or focus of attention. The counterpoint to a fabulous water view, for instance, may be a beautiful inland garden on the opposite side, and illumination from multiple directions helps give any room better energy and balance.

DOING THE RIGHT THING

Finally, the planning and construction of a home is only the beginning of its story. Stewardship is a primary value for Hutker Architects, and we work hard to ensure a long and worthwhile future for our houses. They're the product of an unwavering commitment to thoughtful design, quality materials, and fine craft. We employ energy-efficient technologies, with an emphasis on resiliency and sustainable practices.

As time goes on, we will continue to use emerging insights from the natural, behavioral, and physical sciences to improve our residential space making. Beyond beauty, our goal is to gain a quantifiable understanding of wellness and deploy that knowledge in our work. Our vision is to set a new standard for custom homes to be both passive in their demands on their environment and locality, and active in improving the well-being of their inhabitants.

A NARRATIVE OF MANY STRANDS

Each house we've made is a chapter in a continuing chronicle of design exploration, sometimes taking us as a firm and our clients in directions we couldn't have predicted. So many details and technicalities go into the making of a superlative house—that's a welcome part of the challenge. But even more important is being open to the underlying story of what each home is meant to be, which comes alive in the finished work. Just as our own story as a firm has expanded and developed over time, we want our narrative homes to evolve and change as the years pass, in the hope that they'll continue to resonate with the lives of their present owners and, down the line, become a source of cherished stories for descendants and other residents yet to come.

OPPOSITE: Residential entrances deserve special treatment—in this case, a blackened-steel wall that wraps up onto the ceiling and projects through the front windows to become a porch canopy. In the distance, a beautifully framed exterior view beckons as an interior destination.

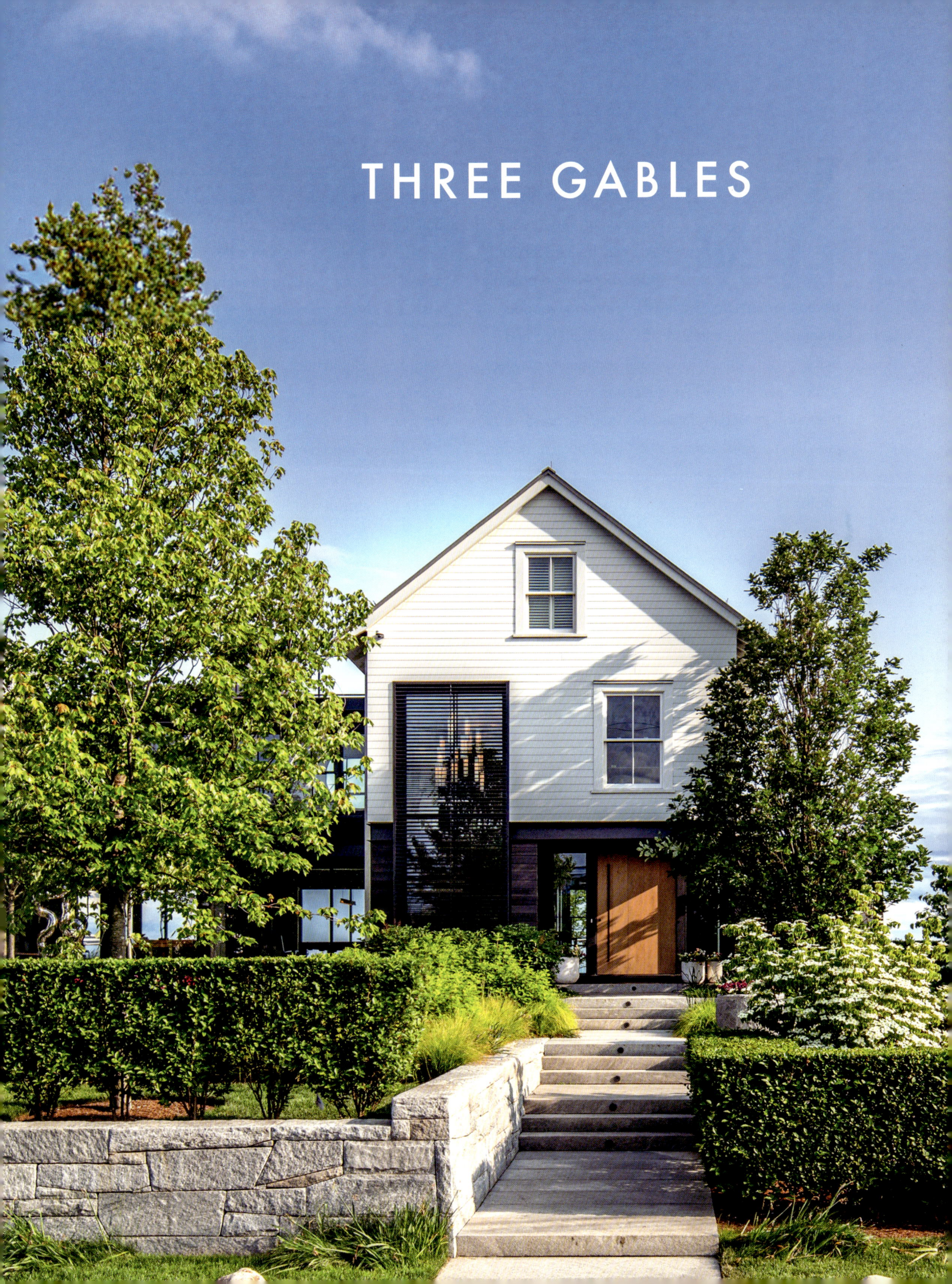
THREE GABLES

Well-to-do oceanfront neighborhoods in New England can vary greatly. One may be a tracery of roundabout lanes—possibly paved, perhaps not—woven thinly among wooded granite bluffs, the estates in it widely scattered and hidden from sight. Another such community may feel somewhat denser, with its succession of grand mansions arrayed in stately rows, each address carefully set apart behind a well-kept fence or hedge.

This locale in coastal Connecticut, is of yet another sort: high-rent but thickly settled, the kind of place where the homes, substantial as they typically are, sit cheek by jowl, all metaphorically craning their necks to maximize their share of the view toward Long Island Sound. Though the neighborhood is private in its way, the houses very definitely coexist—this one neoclassical, this one Tudor, this other one Shingle style—their varied forms contributing to a shared visual environment.

In such crowded and eclectic precincts, how can—how *should*—a new house make its own statement while still fitting in?

Three Gables is situated on an extraordinary lot that backs up right against a seawall and looks out over a full marine panoply of various islands and rocks, a picturesque yacht club, and a well-loved public beach. The street itself, however, is tight, confined by stone walls, and the shape of the property—wide from left to right, quite shallow from front to back—provided real challenges for house making. "We used literally every square foot of development opportunity we could," Mark Hutker recalls. Any time a wall or overhang needed to change during the design process, it meant rethinking the position of some other part of the building to compensate.

The project came with a stylistic complication as well. Accommodating an ambitious list of client wishes and requirements meant that the house would need to be considerably larger than its closest neighbors. But the last thing the owners, or the architects, wanted was to strike a discordant note in the scene. Their solution? Divide and conquer.

The finished dwelling reads as a trio of simple, brightwhite gabled forms, almost like Monopoly houses, embedded atop an ebony base. Two of the white volumes are placed like a resolute pair of bookends, face-on to the street, while the third sits more diffidently off to the side. This high-contrast visual separation "acts as a camouflage," according to firm principal Matt Schiffer. "It breaks up the silhouette of the house so that it matches the scale of the neighborhood."

Obeying the rule of "form follows function," outer changes of shape and material reflect the different uses of the rooms within. The conspicuous gables enclose the family's everyday domestic spaces; the dark clad interstitial areas beneath are where collective social activities happen. A horizontal "belt" of structural steel runs around the home's waist, where the divergent elements join, broken only by the verticals of a central chimney in

PREVIOUS SPREAD: Presented as three white gabled forms cradled in a darker base, the sizeable seaside home comes across as smaller than it actually is. **OPPOSITE:** The house's central section is largely transparent, offering unobstructed views from a street-side sculpture garden straight through to Long Island Sound.

PREVIOUS SPREAD AND ABOVE: Strong statements dominate in the foyer, from a four-foot oak pivot door to a floor paved in hefty Belgian bluestone blocks to the dynamic—and totally scene-stealing—suspended stairway conceived by principal Matt Schiffer.
OPPOSITE: Interior designer Thom Filicia outfitted the central "life room" in a handsome selection of mostly low-slung furniture, the better to highlight the water view beyond the space's oversize glass sliders.

PREVIOUS SPREAD: The home's structural steel skeleton, also visible on the exterior, extends indoors to define the boundaries of the "life room" and an adjacent circulation corridor. A fireplace of stone planks with a steel mantel provides a dramatic central focus for the space.
RIGHT: Gleaming brass outlines the bar set into a side wall, and fiber hangings from Caralarga enhance the framing effect. The room's layout was largely programmed around the homeowner's desire for a pool table.

the rear and a double-height glass panel in the front that allows light into the main stair. (That stair, it should be noted, is a tour de force of dramatic engineering. Suspended from above in a cradle of hollow, one-by-three-inch steel bands, it doesn't actually touch the ground floor.)

"A large part of the concept of the house was trying to make it work from the street side to the water side," Schiffer continues. For one thing, being so close to passing cars and pedestrians created privacy concerns. The Hutker team coordinated with landscape architects to create a raised outdoor sculpture garden that not only screens the residence from traffic but also becomes an alfresco room in its own right when the massive glass doors fronting the central entertaining/billiard space are opened up. In similar fashion, the stairway's lofty glass facing received a protective exterior metal grate that enhances the feeling of security while casting lovely striated shadows inside.

Having climbed from street to front entrance, a visitor continues the journey through to the far wall, where a second array of sliding doors can be thrown wide to the salt-laden breezes. From there begins a beautifully choreographed backyard descent from man-made environment to nature, cascading in a stepped progression from terrace to pool to lawn to seawall—and, finally, to the unbounded expanse of the ocean itself. With front and back walls completely open, the home's upper floors become, in essence, a floating "bridge" connecting the kids' and parents' private domains.

If a site boasts a stellar view, it can be tempting for architects to lavish all their attention on that side of the dwelling—a trap Hutker deliberately avoids. "As infatuating as the view is, you need to look in the other direction," he maintains, "because there are going to be assets there. And when you capitalize on that, you create a better balance." In the case of Three Gables, having the extraordinary front sculpture garden visible in one direction and a prime stretch of shoreline on display in the other ensures a reliable source of pleasure no matter where one's gaze alights.

Finally, sizable as it is, the structure has a twofold identity in terms of function: The linking of the most frequently used household spaces—bedrooms, TV room, kitchen, breakfast area, mudroom, garage—lets it live day-to-day in a surprisingly compact, efficient manner. Then, when company comes to call, it has the resources to give guests a suitably expansive welcome.

Given the right investment of thought and care, the new kid on the block proves to be a respectful participant in the community's architectural conversation: a neighbor with plenty of interesting stories to tell, but never pushy or overbearing. The house achieves what Hutker calls "an essential style, where there's no more and no less than it takes to fit in."

OPPOSITE: Interior warmth comes from the use of highly textured materials throughout the residence. In the dining room these include a Venetian plaster facing for the fireplace and extra-wide planks of wire-brushed French oak laid on the floor.

RIGHT: The bounds of the kitchen, done in collaboration with London's Smallbone, are neatly enclosed by a light-colored soffit that acts as a carrying support for the beamed ceiling. A minimal range hood is suspended underneath, against a backsplash of the same highly figured stone as the extra-thick countertop slabs.

ABOVE AND OPPOSITE: Hutker Architects project manager Ryan Alcaidinho spent countless hours in consultation with the clients, ensuring that the detailing of the primary bedroom and bath—including the stunning room-size shower—was done entirely to their satisfaction. **OVERLEAF:** The rear terraces accommodate several different seating areas as they step down toward the view, in addition to an endlessly long integrated bench, wrapped in tambour-like ipe wood slats, for poolside lounging.

Darker structural sections recede while the lighter ones project forward in relief, adding a beautiful play of shadows to the home's waterfront facade. Two vertically thrusting white granite chimneys—given contrasting metal caps—pin the house to the site in a balanced composition. They are among the very few elements allowed to break the design's overall horizontal banding.

BREEZY POINT

PREVIOUS SPREAD: Twisted oak trees help camouflage a residence that's calculated to be almost invisible from a distance. OPPOSITE: What appears to be the home's front entrance is in reality a sequence of windows looking through the space; the actual door is off to the left. ABOVE: The sculptural black bench, in addition to acting as an important design element, was included as a gift from the architects to the homeowners.

What qualifies as art? The question will elicit a multitude of different answers from different people, and one such answer shaped this Martha's Vineyard house from the ground up. For the family that convenes here every summer, the breathtaking natural landscape is art to the same extent as any painting or sculpture.

The home is hidden away among a row of brackish ponds that jut up like watery fingers poking into the island's southern coast, deep grooves left behind by retreating glaciers. Residential development has reached this section of the Vineyard only recently. During World War II the land was used by the military, and tracts were bought up afterward by a few local families for the purposes of farming and hunting. Even now, neighbors are relatively few, and scattered.

Much of the terrain is flat, with acres of scrubby woods and meadows. It's the domain of what locals refer to as "Vineyard oaks": trees that in any other place would soar, as oaks usually do. Here, however, the salt and the winds mold them into living sculptures, low and gnarled, their branches meandering in the same entrancingly irregular curves seen in Japanese bonsai trees. In the winter, without a softening screen of leaves, they are a powerful presence.

This residence, built at the end of several miles of dirt roads, is as much art gallery as abode, as uniquely adapted to the subtle, understated landscape as are the Vineyard oaks with which it coexists. Views into the building, and from room to room, frame man-made beauty; views out frame the beauties of the biosphere just as carefully.

A fundamental goal, according to Hutker partner Phil Regan, was quite simple: to "weave something in amidst the trees, disturbing as few of them as possible." And if in a few cases the trees happened to stand between the house and the view, it was perfectly okay. They would be respected as an integral—no, *essential*—aspect of that view. (Regan says that only two oaks were cleared during the making of the house, and three were relocated to the property's inland side.)

Seen from across the water, the home's vertical profile is barely detectable—a facet of the design that greatly helped ensure a smooth passage through the town permitting process before construction could begin. The outlying wings and living-dining volume are tucked under low-slung gables connected by the flat-roofed kitchen and circulation spaces. Most exterior walls are sheathed in cedar shingles and planking, whose weathered hues are almost identical to the bark of the surrounding trees. To a casual observer, the house would appear to be almost as rustic as the semi-wilderness it sits in.

And yet, on approach, the opposite gradually becomes apparent. Pulling into a peastone parking circle, arriving visitors are first greeted by a small red barn that does duty as garage, storage, and fitness space. It is a slightly whimsical structure in the same spirit as a garden folly, and an intentional nod to the area's agrarian past. After that, the elegance level

OPPOSITE: The jaunty red barn that greets visitors arriving at the property is a reference to the local community's agricultural past—and, as it happens, also makes a perfect color complement to one of Damien Hirst's "spin" paintings hanging in the living room. Transparent gaps between the slats in the barn's walls allow a welcoming glow to shine through when it's lit at night.

RIGHT: Two long steel I-beams and elegantly slender tie rods support the roof of the living-dining room, and its end walls are sheathed in creamy limestone slabs. A full-width window wall immerses occupants in a view out to the nearby pond.

RIGHT: A thick, bronze-lined threshold leads from the dining area into the kitchen, where flush-mount light fixtures are scattered, starlike, across a cedar-plank ceiling. The range hood is also bronze, and still more bronze outlines the pair of inset cabinets at either side of the doorway.

notches up and up by degrees, as peastone gives way to a tidy boardwalk set between a pair of the carefully preserved oaks, which in turn leads to a formal terrace spread before the front door.

Reaching out like arms embracing this entry sequence are two almost-bare shingled walls; only a single massive plate-glass window breaks each expanse. Centered inside the windows: two choice selections from the owners' prized art collection, as if on display in museum vitrines. In the middle, where the wings converge, a similar large window discloses a view straight through the dwelling toward the open-air tableau on the other side.

The building is laid out in a not-quite-symmetrical sunburst pattern, with multiple wings extending like rays from a main core. In the center are the kitchen, dining room, and living room; the primary suite is in one wing, a guest suite (along with service spaces such as the mudroom, powder room, and pantry) in a second wing, and the third wing accommodates bedroom suites for the family's two sons. Each wing of the house juts out in a separate direction, taking in the scenery from a different perspective. The orientation of each of the home's wings was determined by the sun's daily path. The couple enjoy morning light, so their bedroom faces east; the boys preferred to be on the west, where brightness comes in a little later (but they get killer sunsets); and the public rooms look toward the south, with its prospect of pond, dunes, and beach.

The air of restrained chic is equally evident indoors, as quiet spaces composed of subtly rich materials including walnut, bronze, and pale limestone flow together in a considered procession of experiences. Couture details, like the pencil-thin reveal that demarcates baseboards and window casings from an otherwise pristine wall surface, further the disciplined effect.

Around the home's edges, much care was taken to conserve the maximum amount of indigenous vegetation and finesse the transition from a purely natural ecosystem to more cultivated areas. During construction, the team actually peeled up the existing meadow mat, rolling it back out again when work was done. Where new plantings were needed, landscape architect Kris Horiuchi leaned toward drifts of ferns and similar low-impact interventions.

Regan credits the owners' trust and courage for the stellar success of such an unusual project in a potentially challenging location. Rather than insisting on preconceived ideas of what they wanted their house to be, he says, "they were wide open to doing something that was interesting and something that was unexpected." A very particular slice of nature's bounty called for a very particular vision of placemaking, and both designers and clients rose admirably to the occasion.

RIGHT: An airy breakfast nook adjoins the kitchen. The clients are committed art collectors, and for this house they sought out colorful abstract pieces that felt appropriate to the setting. Strategically placed windows frame views of several exterior oak trees, like the one in the background here, which are uplit after the sun goes down.

OPPOSITE: Glass wraps the southeast corner of the primary bedroom in order to capture morning light and the widest possible expanse of the pond view. The gable roof extends beyond the far wall to shelter a small private deck.
ABOVE: Interior finishes, fittings, and furniture were chosen to suggest a blend of richness and refinement.

The residence sprawls horizontally but rises no higher—not even the chimney—than the surrounding tree canopies. Deep roof overhangs on this southern side act as shields against intense summer sunlight. OVERLEAF: Hutker partner Phil Regan helped the homeowners find the remote property, which looks out over a coastal salt pond, barrier dunes, and the Atlantic. Neighboring conservation land ensures that the area will retain its feeling of seclusion.

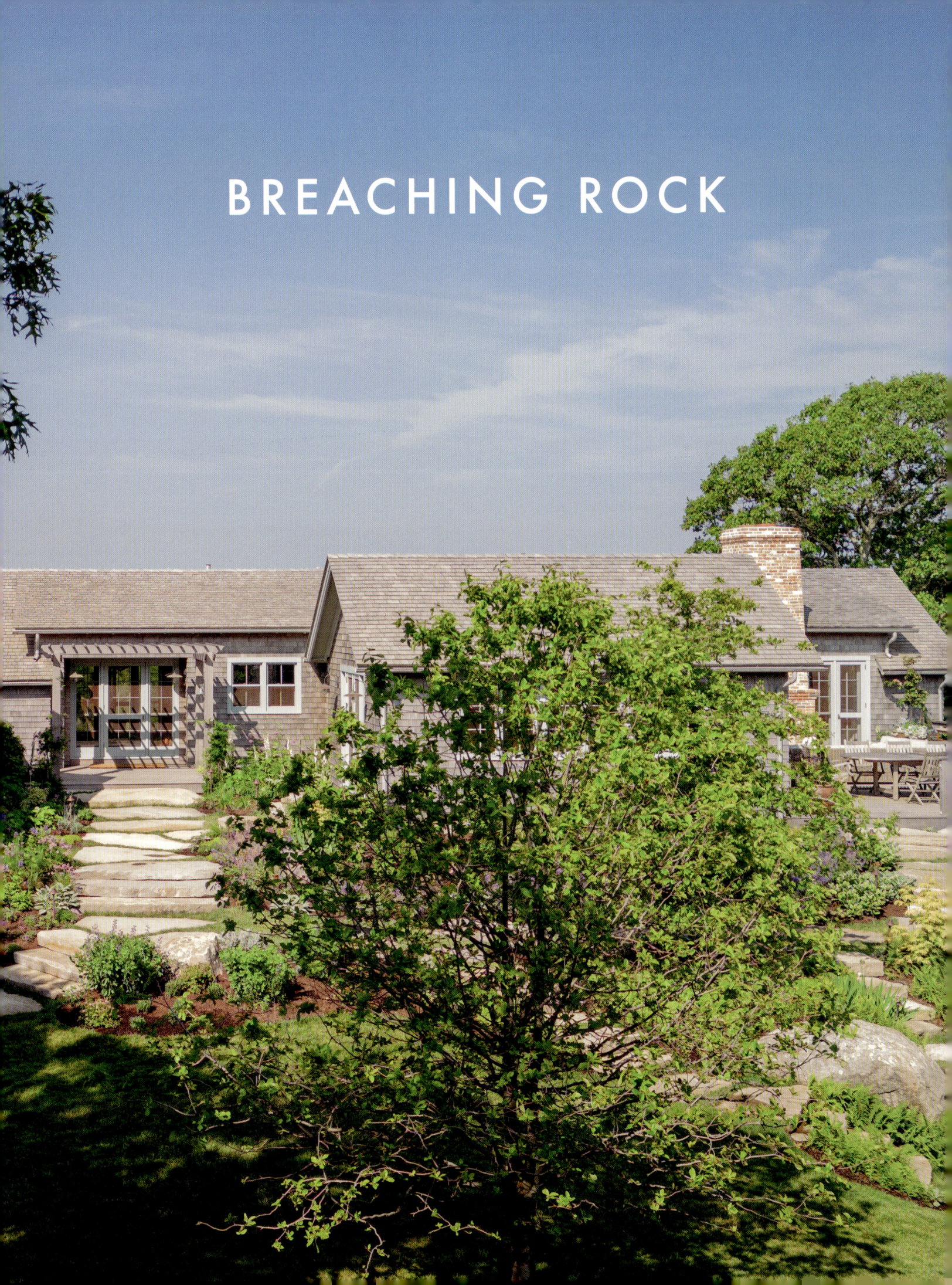

The story of this Martha's Vineyard house sounds at first like a contradiction in terms, or maybe a Zen koan: How do you make something that's actually not what it appears to be, but do so in an authentic way? And consider a second paradox: How does a project undertaken for a client who, at the beginning, is dubious about the power of narrative to shape a home, end up becoming entirely about narrative?

Sheltered deep in the woods of Chilmark and looking toward the island's western end, the property is on hilly terrain, littered with boulders left by ancient glaciers as they departed not quite twenty thousand years ago, at the end of the last ice age. The hefty stones bring to mind the recumbent backs of sleeping cattle, while some of the largest hump up from the ground almost like breaching whales.

An earlier house stood here, an eccentric structure covered in trelliswork and perched on tiptoe, one might say, to capture views out across Lobsterville Beach and Dogfish Bar. New owners bought the place and lived in it for four years or so before connecting with Hutker Architects through a friend of a friend. It was time to put together a home better suited to the family's needs—ideally without forfeiting all of its predecessor's quirky charm.

For each commission the firm takes on, says partner Gregory Ehrman, "We ask ourselves, what's the seed, what's the idea, what's the story? Who is the client and how do they see themselves on this property over time?" The initial answers these questions elicited, in the present case, tended to focus almost exclusively on nuts-and-bolts matters.

As work proceeded, however, a more poetic unifying concept began to coalesce all the same.

Certain priorities were indeed purely practical, although they still benefited from some applied imagination. Because of regulations governing overall height and size for new construction, much of the home's floor space would have to be relegated to its basement. Luckily, the local definition of "basement" includes walk-out areas on a sloped site that need not be entirely underground. So, in an ingenious move, the team enlisted the land's already undulating profile as an ally, heaping up a sizable hillock in order to define a higher grade level for the center of the house—in essence embedding the structure into what appears to be just another natural moraine mound that falls away on either side to give the two ends of the house's lower story both light and air.

As a result, from most directions the home comes across as a pleasantly rambling single-level cottage molded closely to the site, showing a full two-floor profile only when seen from the south. A gradually stepped path that winds through an entry garden smooths out the ascent to the front door— much more gracious than a flight of stairs.

When it came to aesthetics, the question that unlocked creativity was, "What if . . .?" What if, where these two parts of the house meet, the flooring is

PREVIOUS SPREAD: Nestled casually into the landscape, the house looks like a single-story structure despite having two complete, usable levels. A complicated jigsaw of rooflines, along with differing window heights and foundation materials, conveys the impression that it was assembled piece by piece over many decades. **OPPOSITE**: Steps made of irregular granite slabs, designed by landscape architect Kris Horiuchi, lead up in a winding, roundabout approach to the home's entrance.

turned by ninety degrees, as if one piece were built first and this other piece added on later? And what if the rooflines intentionally do not exactly sync up, and one segment of the house—but not the other—is given a brick foundation? Such character-rich oddities, things that might ordinarily look like mistakes in a new house yet could easily happen in an older home that was renovated and enlarged in stages over time, became the defining grammar of the project. Window heights, interior framing systems, and materials change from one section to the next in a progression that is lively and spontaneous, yet always feels purposeful, since the details are generated from the logic of each "historical addition."

Once it emerged, the notion of a "built-in past" spread to influence every detail of design and execution, especially indoors. Vineyard-based builder Mark Hurwitz went all in with period construction techniques and period-appropriate building materials. Everything, inside and out, was made from natural lumber—no recourse to modern engineered wood allowed.

Custom wooden windows were ordered, crafted in historically accurate style with ropes and weights and antique hardware. The cabinetry in the kitchen, baths, and laundry rooms varies in detail, looking as if it had been repurposed from another location or built on-site by local carpenters. Workers were asked not to sand down the rough-sawn wall planking before painting it. Hardware and fittings run the gamut of old-time styles: strap hinges, bin pulls, and wooden knobs in a multiplicity of shapes both painted and not. The drawers in the residence run on felted wooden slides, exactly as they would have a century ago. Most of the light fixtures are antique, rewired and structurally reinforced to meet modern code. Even the art on the walls runs heavily toward local makers, mixed in with found and vintage works that exude a suitably retro ambience.

In the end, a Chilmark homestead that hadn't existed a few years before came into being already trailing a long backstory behind it. It's the kind of place, you feel, that must have belonged to a great-great-grandmother and stayed in the family ever since. "I think it innately has a sense of timelessness," Ehrman says, "because you're not trying to *make* something look old, you're just building it the way it would have been built."

This is no theme-park replica, but an outstandingly functional dwelling that welcomes a twenty-first-century family in full comfort despite origins rooted in past practice. It is a home authentically adapted to its place and time, even if the time in question happens to be both yesterday *and* today.

OPPOSITE AND OVERLEAF: Exposed framing and painted floors create an interior atmosphere that recalls the past even though the house is entirely new. Furnishings and light fixtures, too, were chosen to look collected rather than designed. "Making the intentional look unintentional" was a guiding principle.

Indian chik blinds, bamboo dining chairs, a custom flat-weave rug, and a rough-hewn X-base trestle table combine to give the easygoing dining room a subtly English cast; the model sailboat and bottle lamp are reminders that the ocean isn't far away. Restful blues and greens head up the color palette throughout the house.

OPPOSITE AND ABOVE: Pass-through areas like hallways and the kitchen pantry have flat, boarded ceilings to contrast with the larger cathedral-ceilinged spaces they connect. Period hardware details like wrought-iron strap hinges and painted wood cabinet pulls were lovingly applied to carry through the antique vibe. As the weather changes from season to season, the slightly irregular gaps in the shiplap paneling will expand and contract accordingly.

ABOVE AND OPPOSITE: In the kitchen, an overall rustic look camouflages unavoidably modern amenities such as the range hood as well as luxury touches like honed Carrara marble countertops. The decorative lighting for this project runs toward pendants of many different shapes, sizes, and materials—either refurbished antiques or modern interpretations of classic silhouettes.

PREVIOUS SPREAD: The lower-level family room is eminently lounge-worthy, with its expansive sectional, upholstered ottoman, and medley of throw pillows in (carefully) mismatched fabrics. **OPPOSITE AND ABOVE:** Interior framing systems change from one part of the house to another. In the primary suite, that means visible wall studs as well as rafters. Colors are a bit lighter and calmer here, while an antique clawfoot tub and graceful chandelier add a touch of glamour to the bath.

RIGHT: The cheerful downstairs bunk room can sleep a crowd with its playfully perpendicular arrangement of beds. OVERLEAF: The home's lower level is the heart of the action for younger residents, bringing together bedroom suites, bunk room, and this shared crafting and hangout space. The art selected for this house is a lively mix, with many pieces by Martha's Vineyard–based painters.

ABOVE AND OPPOSITE: Care was taken to preserve the site's many oak trees and lichen-covered boulders—although a few were discreetly relocated—to maintain as much as possible the feeling of undisturbed nature. In addition to providing off-season storage for a vehicle, the car barn accommodates recreational activities like Ping-Pong and the occasional semi-outdoor family dinner.

PREVIOUS SPREAD: Tantalizing glimpses of water visible through the parts of this residence are intended to draw visitors in. Architect Gregory Ehrman likens the separate pavilions to "boulders in a stream: you have to flow around or between them to reach your destination." **ABOVE**: From a rear terrace, the view unfolds in all its glory.

The old house that sat on this bluff, some sixty feet above the waters of Maryland's Magothy River as they begin to merge into the Chesapeake Bay, was a massive, brutalist block of a thing—solid, unfriendly, unapproachable. Which was a real shame, because behind it, if you could hack your way through the overgrown thicket in the back, was an amazing prospect out across miles of glorious terrain, laid out like a diorama in an open-air museum.

New owners, a young couple from Washington, D.C., and their three small children, had bought the plot of land. The family had gotten to know the work of Hutker Architects during summer stays with friends on Martha's Vineyard, and wondered if the firm would consider helping them create something new on this other island a few hundred miles south. Partner Gregory Ehrman and his colleagues, by complete coincidence, had just finished the design of a different house in the same small private community—meaning that they were already familiar with the area and many of the ins and outs of building there. Agreeing to this new commission felt entirely natural to the Hutker team.

The brief for the prospective house was interesting. It would do duty as a summer retreat (golf, tennis, community sailing, and similar seasonal pleasures are on offer nearby). Being within easy reach of Washington, it would also make a perfect destination for shorter, off-the-cuff stays: school vacations, long holiday weekends, maybe even the occasional weeknight. In short, the place needed to be as fit for doing homework in as for hosting Memorial Day pool parties. Intended from the start to be part primary residence and part vacation getaway, it had to combine elements of both.

Given the natural glories of the bluff-top location, all parties knew up front that engaging with the topography and the view would be priority number one. Creating a spacious, relaxed mood was also high on the agenda, as a counterpoint to the family's primary home in a charming but closely packed section of Georgetown.

A cluster of four gabled forms, one of them slightly askew from the rest, now rises among the trees, tantalizing glimpses of distant water and sky visible between and to either side of them. The effect, according to Ehrman, is something like boulders in a stream: not closing sightlines off altogether but forcing the viewer to shift around to take in the full scene. "We wanted the house to envelop you, pull you in right on arrival," he says.

Had the project been located on Cape Cod or Martha's Vineyard, the four pavilions would likely have been joined via a central connector that was at least partially open-air. Mid-Atlantic summers can be punishingly steamy, however, so the grouping was instead tied together with a low-lying, glass-enclosed atrium.

The exterior of the house embodies two complementary, while notably different, personalities, depending on which face you're looking at. Approached from the street, it might best be described as "dapper but reticent"—in keeping with the architecturally conservative community it's part of. Basic shapes are quite traditional. Tidy, white-painted shingles, a shade more buttoned-up than their weathered gray cousins would be, are an equally orthodox choice. Minimal trim and the absence of roof overhangs hint at a taut, tailored modernity, which is heightened by the asymmetrical placement of the (again, very traditional) square, four-light sash windows. A singular, eave-to-ground panel of horizontal planks is an enigma at first; in a delightful surprise move, it turns out to be a huge pocket door that can slide away into the wall on its left, revealing the garage.

Around to the home's rear, walls almost vanish, their expanses replaced by grids of glass and black steel. Add standing-seam metal roofs and the look, though still high style, takes on almost factorylike overtones. Here, the overriding concern was to establish the most intimate possible joining of inside and out.

Indoors, as well, it seems as if a collection of preexisting volumes had been repurposed into a residence. Shingled corners of the taller structures thrust into the flat-roofed center space, with doorways carved out to allow access. The industrial resonance carries through, courtesy of polished concrete floors and exposed structural steel beams used as a modern analogue to a timber frame.

But any illusion of retrofitting is belied by a carefully consistent selection of materials. Luscious, tactile surfaces—creamy plaster, character grade oak with its picturesque knots and varied coloration—balance the harder-edged glass, concrete, and steel. Interior fittings and furnishings lean heavily toward wicker and similar woven substances. A bevy of tribal and botanical patterns in pillows, rugs, and tilework helps ensure that the overall atmosphere is one of bohemian comfort: informal, textured, and a tad raffish.

In the end, a sense of ongoing discovery animates every aspect of the home. "We knew the building was going to be dynamic and respond to the site geometrically," Ehrman says. "And that became part of the character of the architecture once we got going on it."

Intermittent peeks at faraway woods and water afforded by the drive to the neighborhood are merely a foretaste. Being drawn through the entry garden and front door, navigating among the four independent, shifting volumes that combine to form the dwelling, encountering slices of the view and experiencing it differently in different parts of the house as you go, up to the moment when you step out onto the back terrace and immerse yourself in the total panorama—*that* is the true narrative of this special place.

OPPOSITE: A stepped path at one side of the house leads past the pool. The hardscape and plantings were designed by Campion Hruby Landscape Architects to complement the more modern aspects of the home's architecture. **OVERLEAF**: Interior designer Lauren Liess outfitted the airy living room with a variety of enticingly soft and textured furnishings, in contrast to the smoothness of its plaster and structural steel envelope.

An exterior shingled wall slices through into the centrally located dining area. The background stairway leads up to the primary suite and down to a lower-level gym and rec room. Interior colors in the home tend toward a subdued harmony of black, white, gray, and woody browns, with the occasional splash of fresh green.

The kitchen's range hood and backsplash are coated in the same waterproof plaster as the room's walls and ceiling, while an assertive pair of industrial aluminum pendant lights punctuate the space above a cast-concrete island.

OPPOSITE: The wall separating the primary bedroom from its adjoining bath is largely glass, with an opaque central panel where the head of the bed and the bathroom vanity mirrors back up against one another. **ABOVE:** Lively patterned tile animates a guest bath, and a children's bunk room is papered with nautical charts of the community and its surrounding waterways.
OVERLEAF: On its back side, the house becomes almost completely transparent—all the better to connect with the limitless scenery that extends beyond the bluff.

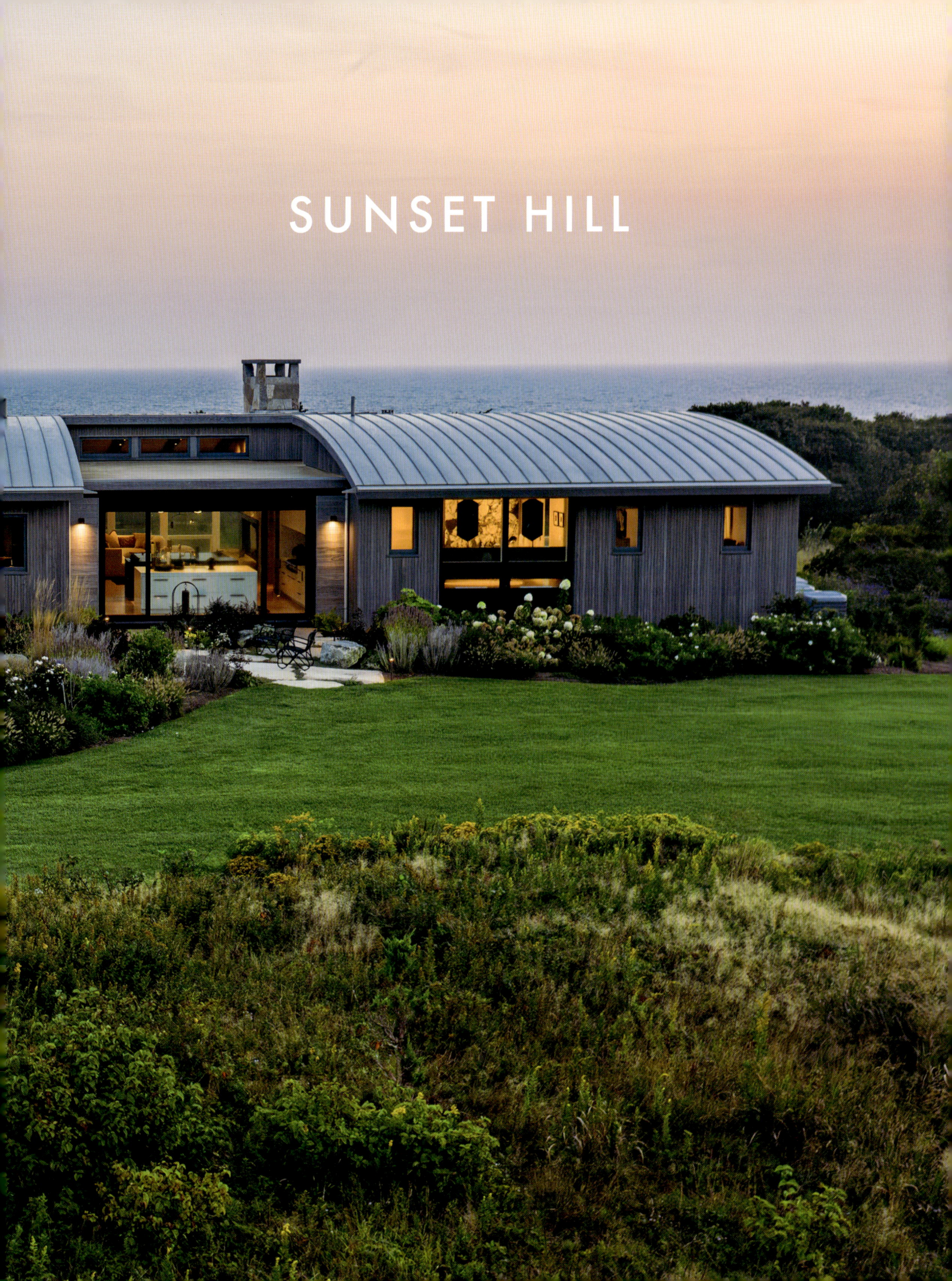

Not everyone, apparently, could see the opportunities offered by the little upland site that had come on the market. Or perhaps they could, and simply had greater concerns about the challenges it might present. At any rate, it seemed that a number of buyers had shied away, assuming they wouldn't be able to do what they really wanted there.

Their hesitancy wasn't altogether unfounded: the town of Aquinnah, on Martha's Vineyard's western tip, is known to be extremely cautious when it comes to development. Aquinnah is also part of the ancestral lands of the Wampanoag people, so many local affairs come under the purview of the town. To further complicate matters, the property in question sits on a slope in plain view of Aquinnah Circle, site of two of the Vineyard's most-visited attractions, Gay Head lighthouse and the Aquinnah Cliffs Overlook. The cliffs are likewise important in Wampanoag religious practice. Any proposed plan for that patch of ground would be sure to draw a great deal of public scrutiny.

Hutker Architects partner Phil Regan, however, felt he had reason to be more optimistic about what might be done on the diplomatically sensitive yet scenically splendid hillside when he was approached by a couple who already owned a house close by. Regan had a long track record of successfully shepherding projects in the town to completion. He'd spent many hours before Aquinnah's Planning Board Plan Review Committee since its inception in 1999, careful to build trust over the years by advocating only for homes he truly believed were considerate of their natural environment and place in the community. The couple, having heard about Regan's involvement in those other projects, asked him to consult on brainstorming some workable options.

They had in mind an abode they could occupy by themselves much of the time but that could gracefully host extended family too. The house should make good use of the site's scenic resources, and its interiors should have a sense of controlled transparency.

As work got underway, the design team gave special attention to anticipating likely issues of review board concern—the handling of scale prominent among them. An old two-story cottage already stood on the site; the proposed replacement, rather than pushing for extra height, would top out a full two feet lower, so that it wouldn't break the tree line on the rise behind it or obstruct views from neighboring houses. Overall mass was disguised even further by employing the frequent Hutker technique of breaking it up into several smaller volumes.

In response to the owners' wishes, Regan cleverly enlisted New England's climate as an ally to give the home variable square footage depending on the season. During the chilly months, when just the couple would be in residence, a relatively compact "primary dwelling" satisfies all of their needs. When visitors come to call in the summer,

PREVIOUS SPREAD: Unexpected in form yet perfectly suited to the gentle swells of its hillside site, the house makes a quietly powerful statement. **OPPOSITE:** A pier-like entry boardwalk extends deep into the structure, ending with a framed view south toward the Atlantic.

they can reside in a separate, secondary dwelling containing extra bedroom suites—at which point a large, stone-paved terrace between the two structures, complete with twin sofas and plunge pool, takes center stage as an outdoor living room, tying the whole architectural ensemble together into a much more expansive, fully equipped family gathering place.

Aesthetic elements were aimed at visual discretion. The existing house had been painted a glaring white; the new one would be clad in planks with a driftwood-like finish, causing it to fade into the landscape. The whole building group was rotated by thirty degrees to minimize solar glare as well as to take maximum advantage of a previously slighted ocean view to the south. This also turned the narrow end of the cluster toward the Circle, further reducing visibility from that direction. Finally, a particularly inspired feature of the scheme was a quartet of elegantly curved, copper-sheathed roof sections meant to appear as if they sprang from the contours of the hill itself.

"We wanted both the house and the hillside to feel comfortable with one another," Regan says, "almost like the individual pieces of the project are a collection of natural objects." In creating the approach to the home, the driveway was reconfigured to snake in from one side to a parking court; from there an entry path winds around the garage and across a foreground meadow to a raised boardwalk, which then continues as an exterior corridor burrowing into the body of the house to eventually reach the hidden front door. Outside and in, the residence unfolds as a series of experiences, areas of interest you can pass through en route toward some object of interest—a sculpture, a stone-and-steel fireplace, a view beyond glass—that stands as a beacon to lead you onward.

Day's end may be the time when the house most dramatically comes into its own. Aquinnah is one of the few places on the East Coast where the sun sets into the ocean; to capitalize on that unique occurrence, windows wrap the western corners of the couple's living room and bedroom, and a private deck sized for two is tucked outside the fireplace wall—perfect for sharing a bottle of wine as the color begins to leave the sky and evening softly falls.

Regan had been convinced that the house would pass muster if its narrative was right. The design didn't sail through review entirely without some grumbling—we're talking local politics, after all—but its evident beauty, growing from a harmonious union of vision and necessity, won approval in the end. A seemingly worrisome lot proved to be nothing of the sort, because both architect and client stepped up to the challenge of open exploration, letting a home be shaped by respect for its site and for its community.

OPPOSITE: The stairs at the right lead up to the primary bedroom and bathroom suite. The wall sculpture is made of stainless-steel bicycle chain. Plaster ceilings in the home almost appear to hover, separated as they are from the walls by an open reveal.

The kitchen's cooking, refrigeration, and storage functions are neatly slotted into side walls of shiplap oak. A darker front island is for dining and socializing; the white island in the rear is geared toward service. Paired glass doors give access to an herb garden outside.

The living room's window wall provides an intimate connection to the outdoors. Furnishings are strong on style but don't compete with the view; for the same reason, lighting for the room is concealed between the curving double rafters.

ABOVE: The client (who is an artist and photographer) oversaw the selection and placement of every stone in the fireplace facade, which floats above a black steel surround. Clerestory windows on the right help balance the room's illumination.
OPPOSITE: The dining room looks across the outdoor "summer living room" toward the secondary dwelling. Over the table, Celestial Pebble pendants from Ochre catch the light even when they're not turned on.

RIGHT: The house is clad in a sustainable, thermally treated wood that is both durable and has a pleasantly weathered look. Landscape plantings are intentionally low-key, meant to integrate visually with the natural meadow growth beyond.
OVERLEAF: The central outdoor terrace, with its comfortable seating and plunge pool, is a favorite family gathering spot at any time of day.

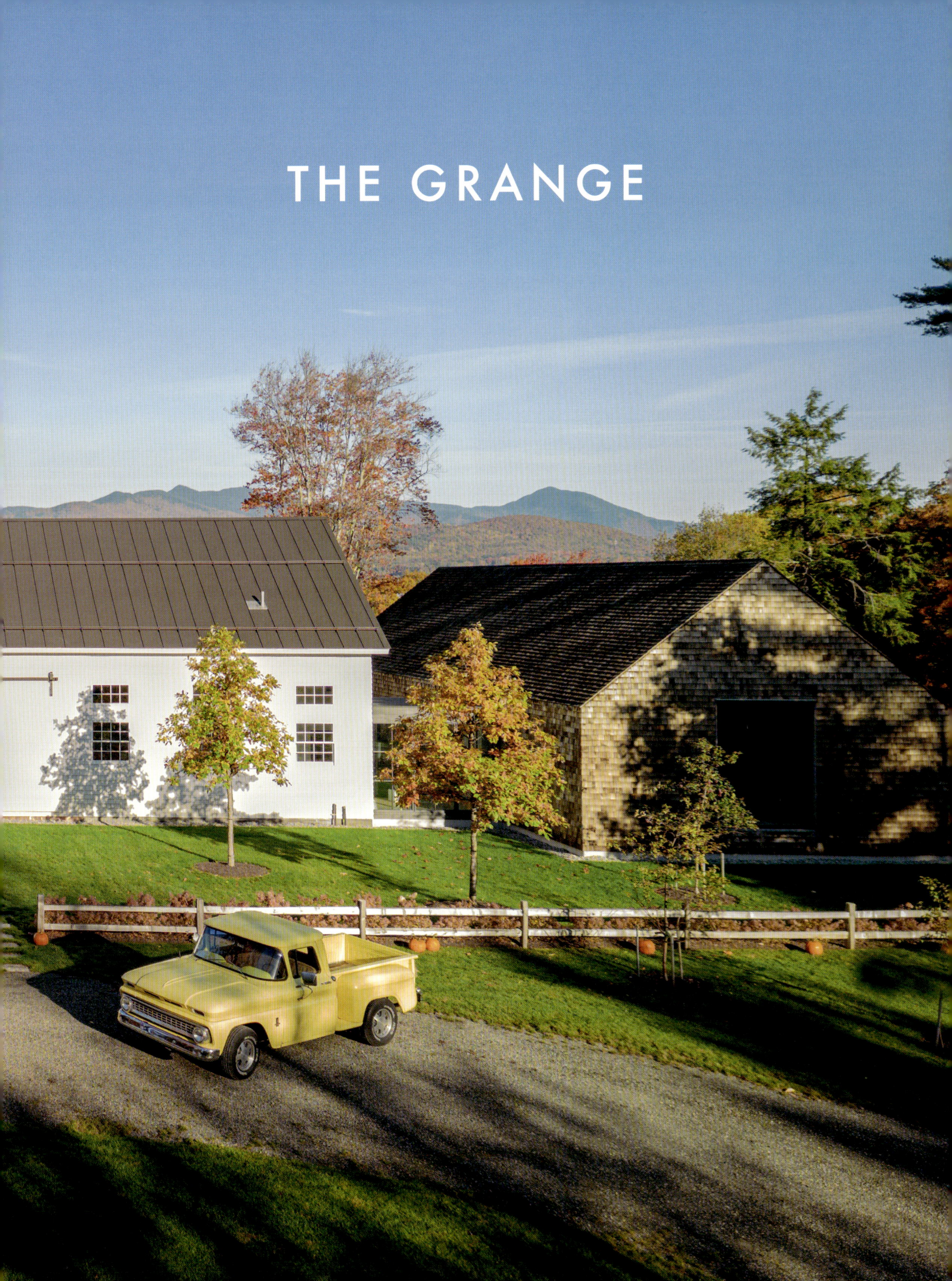

THE GRANGE

Clients' expectations have a lot to do with how house designs evolve. Not just in the obvious sense of "We want a red-brick Georgian," of course, but also in subtler respects of how the design conversation takes place and budgets and schedules are worked out. The owner's perspective sets a fundamental tone that resonates through every stage of a project, from the earliest conceptual parti sketch to the final detailing of a guest bathroom vanity.

The commission for this house in the hills above Stowe, Vermont, came not long after the global pandemic began upending so many aspects of life in the spring of 2020. Its owners, a young Boston couple and their two small daughters, were right on the leading edge of a trend in their decision to repurpose a formerly seasonal dwelling as a refuge away from the city.

A 5,000-square-foot timber-frame structure already stood on the property they had bought. Another 5,000 square feet would have to be added to accommodate the family's list of requirements, including a garage and ski room. Move-in was slated for twelve months after signatures went on the contract; the budget specified was equally optimistic. Neither parameter allowed for much in the way of wiggle room. After some careful consideration, the Hutker team accepted the challenge. With that, a remarkably condensed adventure in creative rebirth was underway.

In terms of raw material, the existing house wasn't entirely ideal. The new owners had a decided preference for calm, white, open rooms, both for living in and as environments for showing off their enviable collection of contemporary art. What then stood on the site, by contrast, was a clunky pseudo-lodge complete with 1980s-era postmodern touches—an overscale, multilevel carport on the front, for one, and a spiral staircase wrapped in glass block inside—plus odd paint colors that, well, hadn't quite stood the test of time.

Its quirky skeleton of rustic, reclaimed timber, on the other hand, held real promise. The task became one of stripping away the less desirable elements of the older building and setting it off against the architectural expansions. Keeping in mind the speed with which the job needed to progress, Hutker partner Gregory Ehrman presented his vision to the clients as a numbered series of concept diagrams, which enabled quick evaluation and approval.

The home today displays a calm, symmetrical, clearly defined face to the world. Its middle segment, the preexisting part, was painted white inside and out, given understated new oak flooring and chaste plaster interior walls, and then outfitted with a metal roof and a pair of sliding barn doors that add gravity to the front entry. Instituting such a pared-down palette of materials and neutral color raises the sophistication level while paradoxically letting the building look more like an authentic bit of agricultural history than it did before. Two straightforwardly present-day additions sit at right

PREVIOUS SPREAD: What appears to be a converted old barn in the hills overlooking Stowe, Vermont, started out as something very different. **OPPOSITE:** "Hyphens" that connect the three main sections of the reconfigured house dramatize the experience of moving from one type of place to another.

ABOVE: Exterior sliding doors installed at the front entry not only add visual emphasis to the center of the building but also permit the home to be closed off when the owners are away. OPPOSITE: When the front doors open, visitors enter the main living area. The existing fireplace was refaced with a new, elegantly curving plaster chimney breast. A raised concrete hearth has room for plenty of wood storage underneath.

A quartet of jumbo baskets used as pendant lights—in addition to being delightfully dramatic—brings the kitchen ceiling height down for a less cavernous feel. Hefty wooden open shelving coordinates nicely with the building's reclaimed timber frame.

PREVIOUS SPREAD, LEFT: Furnishings in the house are relatively few but full of character. Some, such as the circular family dining table, are sleek and modern; others are rough-hewn. PREVIOUS SPREAD, RIGHT: A larger dining area meant for company not infrequently doubles as a gaming and project construction space for the children. THIS SPREAD AND OVERLEAF: The library is the one room where a strong color is allowed to dominate, from walls to shelves to invitingly cushy sectional sofa.

angles on either side, forming a large *H*. Glass "hyphens" stitch the three pieces together.

In its previous lodge form, the residence lumped together public and private spaces as a single unit. An important goal of the Hutker redo was to create some separation between guests, parents, and children. The central barn remains the locus for shared living (with a guest suite sequestered upstairs) but has now been augmented with private domains in the twin wings. The transparent breezeways stand out as thresholds between those two realms, enforcing, by a brief pause, the sense of movement from one architectural place to another.

This organizational scheme will continue to support the household over time as the children grow, become increasingly independent, and perhaps eventually start families of their own. For example, the space presently set up as an office is equipped with a full bath, so it can be repurposed when needed as an extra bedroom suite; the current guest suite can also be taken over by family members if necessary.

Antique versus new is the visual theme that matches the functional narrative, with two clearly contrasting languages defining the barn and its flanking gables—although on second glance the rustic-refined divide is more nuanced than it initially seems. The differentiation in style is as much a matter of line and proportion as anything else. Similar materials are used throughout the home, a streamlined syntax being the chief indicator of modernity—such as when the weathered cedar shingles on the twin wings just fold up onto the roof sans any intervening cornice or eave. Divided-light windows are employed in both contexts, but at greatly different scale and with either light- or dark-colored frames to emphasize or minimize the separation of the panes. Indoors, as well, the family spaces have their own reclaimed timber accents, except fined down to an elegant slenderness. The trick, Ehrman says, "was finding the right amount of borrowing, so there are threads that pull the looks together."

Only in the rear, where the primary bedroom and owners' office open out to an echt-Vermont tableau of rolling, forested hills and Mount Mansfield in the distance, does the house dispense with history. It's as if the gable ends were sliced off, open to the landscape, and only grudgingly filled in with glass as a concession to the weather.

Whatever uncertainty the team might have had at the project's start, everything came together as planned. ("It was incredible," Ehrman confides. "Design, permitting, construction, move-in: all within a year.") The finished home now has an admirable clarity, a Shaker-like calmness of barn-turned-art gallery, making it a place where people simply want to be and an accurate reflection of its owners' intent.

The visual evidence leads to a final verdict: nothing here feels rushed or looks like anything less than a luxury production, which is the greatest indication of success. And the clients' personal goal for a family refuge came to fruition.

OPPOSITE: Extensions on the back ends of the home's two wings shelter private decks—this one serving the primary bedroom and the other attached to a private office.
OVERLEAF: The homeowners wake up every morning immersed in Vermont's mountain scenery.

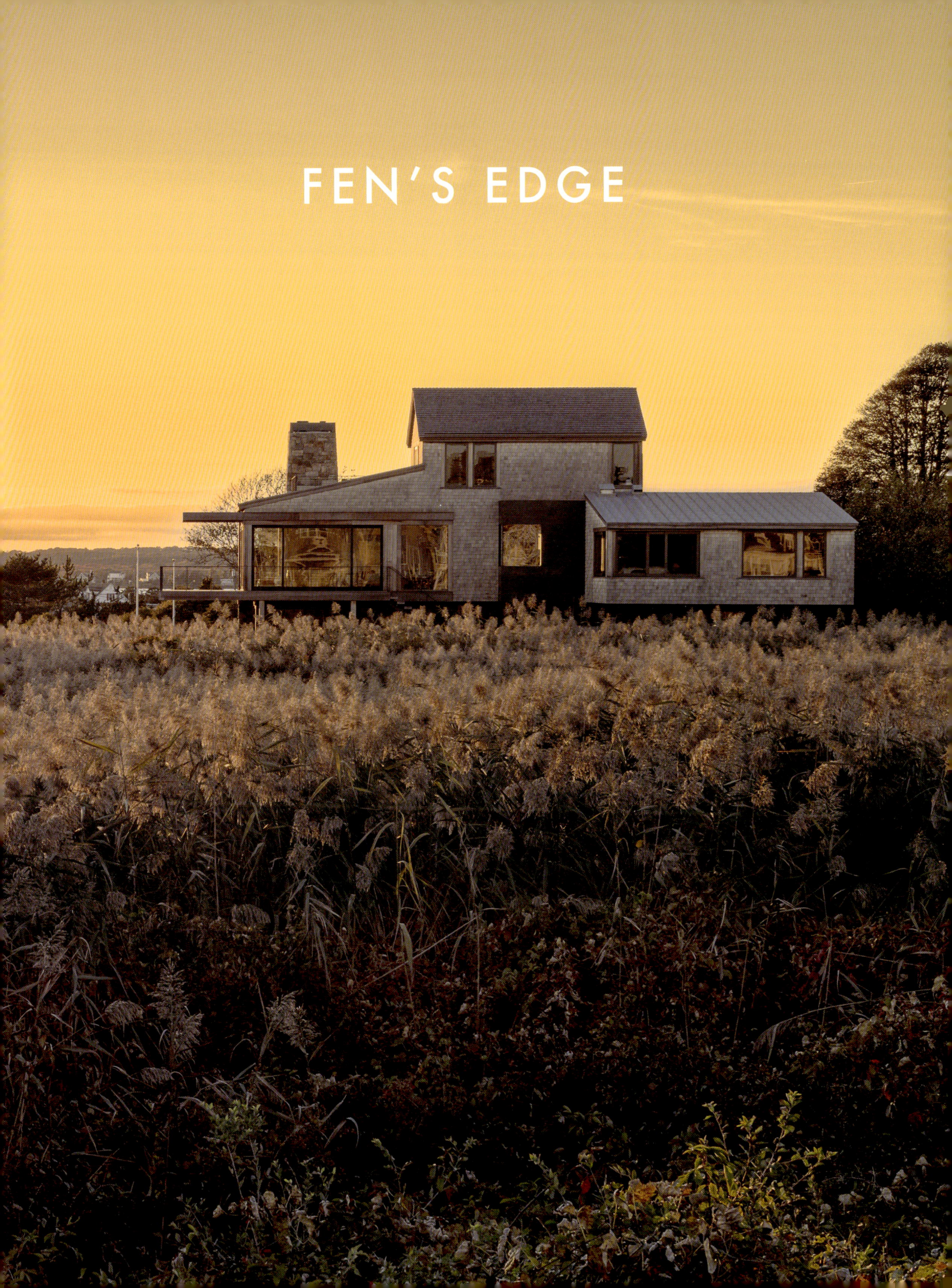
FEN'S EDGE

Located on the Rhode Island coastline, Fen's Edge is a home that may seem unassuming at first, but it represents a steady accumulation of perfectly calibrated details. The structure's cleverly interlocked assembly of residential and landscape spaces is quite moderate in scale (only three bedrooms, for example), yet it functions well beyond its physical size, and its exquisite tailoring becomes more and more apparent the longer you look.

The house is built on an extremely deep, narrow lot that was formerly occupied by a Victorian cottage similar to many others in the vicinity. Its owners—a couple with European roots and their adult son—had in fact been spending weekends and summers in that cottage for years, getting by well enough. But eventually they knew it was time to make an abode of their own, one that could be fine-tuned just for them.

"Our clients wanted something more contemporary than the houses that existed around them," says Hutker partner Thomas McNeill. "It was a challenge for us, because we needed to fit it into the community and still push the limits a little bit beyond the usual." Victorian and Shingle-style homes tend to have a high, central section, with a gabled roof turned end-on to the street and lower porches attached to the front and sides. The scheme of the new house, therefore, follows suit: a tall gable is accompanied by two horizontal, shed-roofed companion volumes. Although distilled down to essential geometry, forgoing nineteenth-century decorative flourishes, the overall silhouette and mass of the dwelling remain very much in character for the neighborhood.

One unique natural blessing of the site made real magic possible. Coming at the end of a row of similar properties, the parcel abuts a pocket of marshland covered in *Phragmites australis*, otherwise known as the common reed. An aggressively invasive wetland grass, it is also an undeniably appealing one, particularly when masses of its crowning plumes surge and ripple in the wind. Having a fen next door allowed the architects to open up the home's whole flanking facade, taking in an abundance of sunlight and scenic prospects unlike any others in the immediate area. The primary rooms inside are oriented toward those views, eastward across the marsh and south across the street to the waters of Block Island Sound. In many cases, broad picture windows wrap around a corner to provide an uninterrupted panorama in both directions.

Seen from afar, the upper reaches of the house appear to float, ship-like, atop grassy waves, while its lower level disappears beneath them. McNeill enhanced the effect by sheathing the submerged bottom story in shadowy Japanese-style *yakisugi* charred planks. The ocean of reeds, poetic as it is, also serves as a practical means of camouflage for a sequence of outdoor amenities—a Zen garden, dining terrace, and pool—screening them from the daily parade of neighbors passing by in transit to and from a nearby beach. The property manages to be attached to the public realm and notably private at the same time.

PREVIOUS SPREAD: Like a ship sailing on a sea of tasseled reeds, Fen's Edge appears to float off toward the sunset.
OPPOSITE: The approach to the residence runs alongside the pool. Landscape architect Katherine Field divided off areas of plantings with low Cor-Ten steel walls.

The materials palette chosen for the house is another key contributor to its unshowy mien. Four basic substances—wood, stone, bronze, and glass—define the entire composition. (The liberal use of bronze, as it happens, had a personal resonance for the owner, who is involved in copper mining.) Mark Hutker calls it "a modern way of thinking about how to build," which "makes a lot of decisions for you as you design," leading to an outcome that, though spare of means, is rich in effect.

A stone retaining wall cradles the back of the building, then extends full-length on the border overlooking the marsh, separating human habitation from nature. There's only a single calculated break in the masonry: an outdoor shower, executed in opaque glass and the same fire-treated cladding as the lower level of the house, hangs dramatically out over the wetland, creating an unforgettable experience for those who use it.

Low Cor-Ten steel walls—suitably rugged analogues to the bronze accents used in the house proper—make up the pool enclosure and wrap around a circular firepit. Rougher granite paves the meditation garden, while the outdoor dining room is floored with slabs recovered from a centuries-old terrace in China. ("You can actually see wear on the stone from being walked on," McNeill says.)

Packing a great deal of living potential into a not-so-big space was one goal for the project, as was respectfully fitting a modern residence into a traditional seaside town. Unassuming and apparently artless as it may be at first glance, to experience this house is to appreciate the nuances of subtle perfection. "There's a simplicity to it that is really mature and knowing," Hutker observes. "I would say that the spaces are very modest, but there's an immodesty to the detail and the beautiful craft with which things are put together."

Can that really count as immodesty? If so, it's a sin with which it's hard to find much fault.

PREVIOUS SPREAD AND OPPOSITE: Wraparound windows, with low-visibility cable railings on the deck outside, make the relatively compact living room feel more capacious. Set into the stone chimney breast, a slightly tilted bronze panel surrounds the firebox. The furniture selections by Colorado-based interior designer Catherine Frank have a midcentury-modern cast.

Spaces for living, dining, and cooking flow easily and naturally into one another. Ambient lighting and HVAC systems are all recessed within and around the edges of the wood ceiling.

As with other sections of the house, blackened bronze is used to outline windows and other structural elements of the kitchen. The corrugated detail on the edges of the island's waterfall stone top and the conspicuous grain of the oak cabinets contribute welcome texture.

Wraparound windows also enlarge the experience of the primary bedroom, with the bed itself recessed into a more sheltered-feeling paneled niche. The sloped ceiling comes courtesy of a shed roof above.

Glass partitions allow light to flood all parts of the primary bath, shower stall and water closet included. In the back wall, a playfully placed window looks out between the his-and-hers sinks.

FROM LEFT TO RIGHT: Changes in the alignment of the primary bathroom's limestone flooring are strategically placed to help define different functional areas—such as the bay that holds a soaking tub. A rooftop deck affords a terrific view of the nearby beach and Block Island Sound. Shifts in material that denote alterations in architectural structure also happen on the exterior of the home. The outdoor shower is as much a jewel box as the house itself.

BIG BLUFF

Sometimes the story of a house begins long before its actual construction. In this instance, it began more than a century before. The story is about a community on Martha's Vineyard. The neighborhood is a historic one, with tennis courts and plenty of social events and sailing sponsored by the local yacht club. It's the kind of place where residents keep rockers on the front porch from which to wave and greet the scores of folks who will be walking or biking past during their evening promenade.

Strung side by side along the waterfront, like gulls facing the wind, is a series of Shingle-style and Victorian homes that Mark Hutker refers to as "the Gray Ladies." These are homes "that have grown over time," he says. "They've experienced a lot, they've nurtured their families a lot, and they've nurtured the community a lot."

A family that had summered in the area for many years was fortunate enough to find one of these houses—known as Big Bluff—on the market, and snapped it up, furnishings and all. They then secured the services of Hutker Architects to help create a place where they could carry tradition into the future.

Lifestyles and building technologies had changed over one hundred–plus years, of course, enough so that a simple reworking of the original home turned out not to suffice. Big Bluff's new owners, though—and their architectural firm—were determined not to let go of the qualities that made the dwelling special. Before the old structure was torn down, principal Matthew Cramer and other members of the design team went through it, carefully studying its details and rescuing pieces of furniture to be refinished or repainted and used afresh.

Today's Big Bluff is bigger than the one that was there before, but the architects broke up its volume, visually speaking, into multiple segments to help maintain a scale commensurate with the neighborhood. What appears to be an older, gambrel-roofed central section has had "additions" put on at each end, including a generous screened porch. Weighty, painted-brick chimneys appear at some of the "joins," just as they would have if the whole arrangement had evolved naturally over time. An ell on the rear accommodates, among other things, a garage and upstairs bunk room.

The lot is wide laterally, yet more restricted from front to back, and enjoys a first-class, 180-degree view of Vineyard Sound across the street. For that reason, much of the house is only one room deep, the main public spaces lined up like train cars with an open corridor on either side for easy circulation.

The two front doors (a "social front door" on the water side and an "owners' front door" on the land-facing side) open into a center stair hall that also serves as the main dining room, complete with a baronial fireplace. To one side is a comfy library that these days gets much use as a pleasant setting for hunkering down over a laptop. To the other side is the "life room," combining kitchen, breakfast niche,

PREVIOUS SPREAD: Although it replaced an earlier home in the same location, the new Big Bluff was careful to respect the historical ambience of its neighborhood. OPPOSITE: Landscape architect Dan Gordon marked the approach to the inland "owners' entrance" with a rhythmic bluestone walk and a curved arbor.

bar, and family room into one stylish and highly functional package. Triple-panel sliding doors on both sides of a beach-stone fireplace can retract entirely, adding the screened porch as an integral part of the room in good weather.

On the second floor, the rooms are arranged so that they all get their share of light, air, and ocean vistas, including the primary bedroom suite, husband's office, and a multitude of additional sleeping quarters for visitors and children. Once you ascend the stairs, oak floors give way to less formal painted wood and the millwork details in each space are slightly different. One bedroom may sport a "shell shelf" up near the ceiling. Another has built-in nooks for luggage. And in one more, the closet is screened off by a pin-striped curtain rather than a wooden door. Each detail is lovingly re-created from local models of period building.

Throughout the home, the Hutker team's command of New England vernacular style and their affection for the island's traditional ways is clear. "Carpenters built these houses—there weren't a whole lot of designers drawing interior elevations back then," Hutker explains. While drawing plans, "we often ask, 'What would a Yankee carpenter do?' A Yankee carpenter would have done *this*, it would have been *so* simple, and it would have had a lot of logic to it. And that's what I love about it."

Interior design in this home is approached in the same spirit. Vintage pieces saved from the old house are judiciously mixed with furniture of more recent silhouettes, with light fixtures in particular trending toward modern forms. Floor coverings are a definite source of drama, sporting motifs drawn from quilting and other such conventional patterns but often magnified to a larger, twenty-first-century scale. All told, however, the goal is never to depart too radically from how the rooms would have felt back in the early 1900s.

Despite the fact that it was designed intentionally and executed all at once, this is a house that feels and lives like it evolved in its surroundings. "The other 'Gray Ladies,'" Hutker says, "they've all changed too. They had pieces taken off and new pieces put on, and garages and carriage houses were added to the properties. All of this happened over time, and it's what adds to the richness and uniqueness of the neighborhood."

As an indicator of continuity—a sign that even if the materials are new and the systems perform to contemporary standards, the important thing, the vision of gracious seaside life, has stayed the same—the house continues to be known as Big Bluff. And the reborn Big Bluff is a worthy successor to the much-loved abode that formerly stood in its place.

OPPOSITE: The central stair hall doubles as a formal dining room. The Hutker interiors team outfitted the home in a classic palette of blue and white with red accents. **OVERLEAF:** A beach-stone fireplace with an inset driftwood log for a mantel provides a visual center in the "life room." Telescoping doors on both sides can be thrown wide open to the screened porch beyond.

ABOVE: The kitchen range hood has a shallow arc that echoes the home's front facade. **OPPOSITE:** A cheerful breakfast nook artfully combines old with new, including a built-in banquette and mismatched chairs. **OVERLEAF:** Much of the kitchen woodwork, such as the glass-fronted upper cabinets resting on graceful curved brackets, is based on a study of period models.

ABOVE: The primary bedroom's window wall was designed to act as a sort of extended headboard for the bed, and shiplap paneling gives the space a less formal feel than the rooms downstairs. The two nightstands are among the pieces of furniture rescued from the old house. OPPOSITE: In the primary bath, a soaking tub is placed on a raised platform just high enough to let bathers easily see the ocean outside.

ABOVE AND OPPOSITE: Each of the second-floor bedrooms incorporates a different riff on early twentieth-century carpentry details. Some of the antiques were manufactured by a furniture company that once existed nearby. Even when the decorative lighting fixtures are modern, painted floors and a mix of patterned textiles keep the overall look decidedly traditional. **OVERLEAF:** Several different porches, equipped with slat-back rockers and comfy wicker, invite relaxed contemplation of the Vineyard Sound view.

LEDGE HOUSE

PREVIOUS SPREAD AND ABOVE: The various pavilions of this house in suburban Greenwich, Connecticut, are organized around a rectangular front courtyard, based on the owner's love of Argentinean courtyard homes. An open fireplace sits at the center point of the street-side wall, offering a warm sign of hospitality when lit. All of the stone employed in construction was sourced from the site itself.

The architectural history of Greenwich, Connecticut, and the family and food culture of Argentina are probably not subjects you'd expect to be paired. Traveling along one of the Fairfield County town's pleasantly wooded residential lanes, though, you can find a house that does, in fact, have ties to both.

In the heart of an area overflowing with Georgian pediments, white-painted clapboards, and similar hallmarks of Colonial style, the dwelling known as Ledge House instead shows the street a face of chunky, irregular gray-brown stone and weathered cedar planking. Only partially visible behind a row of flowering trees, a parking court, and a head-height wall, its barnlike pavilions could easily be mistaken for relics of the area's agrarian past.

The stone employed here has most definite— quite literal—local roots, but the animating vision for the property, not so much.

"The family comes in part from Argentina and has a strong affinity for Argentinean culture, lifestyle, and cooking as well," says Hutker partner Thomas McNeill, "which inspired us to look at all sorts of different ways Argentinean houses were created." Because the site fronts a relatively busy road, a South American courtyard house quickly stood out as the ideal model to emulate.

Consequently, the Connecticut residence is set back from the street, screened off from traffic behind a grassy quadrangle. One edge of the expanse is defined by a garage; on the others, stone walls reach out to complete the enclosure. The home remains connected to the public realm, but at a slight remove. ("We're adding layers of privacy as you come up toward the house" is how McNeill describes it.) Lest the arrangement seem forbidding, however, the architects included an especially unique and memorable feature: a see-through fireplace sits at the very center of the outer courtyard wall, facing the street, casting a glow that assures arriving visitors a warm welcome.

Greenwich has long been known for its difficult terrain. Solid granite ledge rock lies beneath a thin coating of soil, often poking up in humps and dramatic outcroppings. General George Washington complained bitterly during the Revolutionary War about the toil of moving troops and artillery through the innumerable stone walls farmers had piled up at the edges of their laboriously cleared fields.

The Hutker team saw its site's geology as both a challenge and an opportunity. A great deal of ledge would need to be excavated before construction, and the process would produce a lot of loose stone. On the other hand, this was the same stone that had been used in previous centuries to erect many churches and other civic buildings in the town center—so why not do the same thing today?

The builder, Cum Laude Group, rigged up a custom-made sieve to filter out all the dirt and debris after blasting. The separated rock was then broken into usable pieces and employed to construct the various stone elements of the architecture: garage, courtyard walls, gable-end facade, chimneys. In the end, almost no excess had to be carted away.

The premium Argentinean society places on communal family life greatly influenced the functional layout of this house. Its three main volumes form a rough *H* shape, joined together by a pair of glassed-in walkways. Much of the center crosspiece is dedicated to entertaining, in an expansive first-floor space that combines formal dining room, living room, and billiard room. The owners' primary suite is upstairs. The wing to the right encloses a well-appointed guest or in-law suite and sitting room, as well as the husband's office. The left-hand wing is entirely dedicated to the core household: kids' bedrooms upstairs, and shared areas (mudroom, pantry, kitchen, informal dining area, family room) on the ground level.

Perhaps the most obvious import from the Southern Hemisphere stands in the backyard, next to the pool and attached to the family wing. The *quincho* is a mingled outdoor kitchen and socializing space used for *asado*, the traditional Argentinean barbecue. Typically occurring at least once a week (often on Sunday), it's an hours-long, whole-family-and-friends event revolving around an abundance of side dishes and tons of meat cooked on a specially designed grill.

As is almost universally true in Hutker-made homes, nearly every part of the interior is given an intimate link with the outdoors. Wide glass expanses on the front and back of the central entertaining space can slide away into the walls, opening up an unobstructed path from the forecourt straight through the house to the rear lawn. Hallways and other axes of circulation invariably end in some kind of visual goal, be it a scenic view or a work of art. The connecting glass "hyphens" dramatize the act of moving within a landscape from one architectural volume to the next.

Farmhouse-derived elements inside, including barn doors and rustic ceiling beams, add a comfortable informality and texture and harmonize with the historic-seeming exterior. The reigning ambience, all the same, is never less than sophisticated and modern.

"Sometimes we take cues from the context and the neighborhood to inform what a house should be," McNeill says. "This house takes authentic cues from the neighborhood but doesn't try to match." The cues for this home were pulled from the earth it sits on, the history of the town it's in, and the character of the family that lives in it. Different as it may look on the surface, in its essence it couldn't be a truer reflection of place.

OPPOSITE: A steel wall and ceiling accent the home's main entry. In the background, decorative clay tiles set into the wide-plank French oak flooring signpost the transition to a different part of the residence.

The central entertaining space combines areas for formal dining, lounging, and billiards. Beyond a library that backs up to the home's entryway, a steel-and-oak staircase leads up to the family bedrooms.

A massive cantilevered island holds pride of place in the kitchen. The wood used for the dining bar came from oak trees blown down by Hurricane Sandy. OVERLEAF: Two separable tables in the breakfast nook, made of the same oak, allow easy access to an extra-long custom bench designed by the architects.

OPPOSITE: The parents' suite is sequestered on the second floor of the central pavilion, although it has easy access to the children's wing via an upstairs connector. Window seats on either side of the fireplace look out over the backyard.
ABOVE: The primary bath comes equipped with its own built-in upholstered seat facing the tub. Ceiling beams throughout the house were reclaimed from a barn in Virginia.

ABOVE AND OPPOSITE: A private office sits at the front of one side pavilion. The double-height space holds a custom-built desk, and layered cowhides provide textural interest underfoot. The huge granite block along one wall acts as a hearth for one of the house's many Rumford fireplaces. A stretch of garden outside is screened away from the street for solitude.

The family room, adjoining the kitchen and overlooking the backyard pool, is where everyday life tends to happen. A close integration with the landscape is cultivated in most Hutker rooms. The steel framework around the fireplace also outlines a bookshelf and a niche for storing firewood.

OPPOSITE: The *quincho*, or Argentinean outdoor kitchen, includes an adjustable wood-fired grill and a pizza oven. **ABOVE:** Drop-down screens are hidden around the perimeter of the outdoor living room. **OVERLEAF:** A large hump of the property's underlying ledge rock, visible at left, adds character to the backyard. As time goes on, different parts of the cedar planks sheathing the home will weather to different hues, based on their degree of exposure to the elements.

GREAT POND

Many of humankind's most cherished stories—from early epics such as *Gilgamesh* or Homer's *Odyssey* to, more recently, *The Lord of the Rings*—have revolved around fateful journeys. As any reader of these tales knows, they tend to share a common scheme: the main character decides on a goal, chooses companions for the quest, faces a series of trials, and—at least most of the time—triumphs in the end. Ask about the history of one striking house at the southern edge of Martha's Vineyard, and the answer you'll get is a triumphant recounting of that same sequence.

Great Pond's owners are a retired couple with adult children and grandchildren also on the island; they raised their family there and have been deeply enmeshed in the community for decades. Not long ago, they concluded that it was time to make a special place just for the two of them—somewhere their whole brood could enjoy visiting, sure, but mainly a personal haven to settle into and relish coming back to after their frequent travels.

Selecting partners to help realize their vision turned out to be an almost effortless process. Both husband and wife had met members of the Hutker Architects team while serving on the boards of several local nonprofits. "They knew about us, they followed our work, and so they just approached us and announced, 'We're ready to do our house!'" Gregory Ehrman remembers with a laugh. "It was the most natural pairing ever." And so the intrepid travelers set off.

The property where the building would rise originally extended over many acres. Various chunks had been carved off through the years, however, and what remained was a low-lying parcel facing south across a serene, horizontal expanse of tidal pond, with a barrier beach in the distance and then nothing but the Atlantic Ocean extending all the way to the horizon.

Wonderfully scenic as the site was, it posed challenges. A very small house was already hunkered down amid the marsh grasses. Because of its proximity to the water, zoning regulations would only allow a replacement residence to be 10 percent larger, yielding a final figure of barely more than 1,700 square feet. And with global sea levels on the rise, long-term resilience would be a second concern; among other things, a new structure would have to be elevated significantly.

Luckily, the couple was fine with something small. Although this would be their primary residence, their wish list was modest. Both are creatives—he has worked in lighting design for Hollywood films; she is a painter and quilter—so the final program for the dwelling included a studio for each of them, in addition to just one bedroom suite, living room, dining room, and kitchen (plus an outlying garage and storage shed). The pair were equally inclined to lean in on the environmental front, aiming for a home that would still be sturdy and useful fifty to a hundred years hence and resolving, in fact, to build a certified passive house.

In essence, grappling with those many constraints is what drove the architects' design

PREVIOUS SPREAD: A delicate coastal ecosystem required careful handling in the placement and design of this house. Despite some rustic-seeming features, the building incorporates a good bit of high-performance engineering.
ABOVE: The artistic disposition of masses gives Great Pond a surprisingly imposing architectural presence for such a compact dwelling. **OVERLEAF:** A gently slanting ramp leads through an arrival garden to the front door; once inside, visitors are greeted by a pocket-size tiled foyer.

OPPOSITE: The home's central circulation space is also its dining room. The irregular frame around the built-in hutch at right is modeled on a motif from the owner's quilting work. ABOVE: A welcoming sectional sofa in the living room faces the view. OVERLEAF: Narrow windows sandwiched between the blocklike floating modules of the house frame slices of the outdoors like vertical landscape paintings.

process. The house has to be raised up nearly six feet, so what if we make it float above the dune grass? If all of the rooms must be super-compact, how about we play up their separateness and the drama of moving from one to another?

The end product features a central core, set under a gabled copper roof, which does double duty as both dining room and circulation space. Then the other program elements project out from its sides as flat-roofed, levitating rectangular blocks. Visitors reach the front door in stages by way of a raised arrival garden and a shallow ramp—an active progress through the landscape that is much more appealing than simply mounting a flight of steps.

When it comes to aesthetics, the clients greatly admire Japanese *wabi sabi*, which looks for the beauty hiding in imperfect, impermanent, or incomplete things. Thus, materials, finishes, and construction techniques were chosen for their expressive potential. The raw structural steel framing the home's central volume is completely visible, given a simple oil rub to bring out its surface irregularities. The kitchen cabinets are clad in rough sawn reclaimed wood, showing all the marks left by the whirling blade. Changes in texture denote differences in function. Where they pierce a wall to continue inside, the living room, kitchen, bedroom, and studio cubes sport an outer skin of wooden planks, while the surfaces within them are coated in smooth, white plaster. Outdoors, foundations and raised landscape elements are encased in Cor-Ten, a weathering steel whose rusty patina grows only richer with the years.

Hitting just the right balance of art and science was the fundamental task in this home-building epic—playing off the hardheaded calculations required to achieve passive certification against, say, the desire for a few more inches of window to take in the seductive water view. (Ultimately the home produces more energy than it uses; the excess is sent through the grid to the couple's children across town.) The design's fitness will shine through over the long haul in the ease with which it promotes the comfort and health of its occupants and the understated elegance with which it inhabits its setting.

In making a new house, "there's wayfinding, there's discovery, there are moments of being unsure," says Ehrman. "We don't know where we're going to end up, either. This is a journey that we're doing together." But—as in all the best stories—with trust, goodwill, a sense of adventure, and the right band of comrades, there's sure to be a victory waiting at the end of the road.

PREVIOUS SPREAD AND ABOVE: Luckily, energy-efficient passive house requirements allowed the south-facing kitchen to enjoy a broad ribbon of windows overlooking the pond. The role of textural pattern is especially noticeable in this room, as rough-cut boards change directions on different sections of the cabinetry. Symbolic bronze cutouts with special meaning to the family are embedded into the side of the kitchen island; the metal plate from which they were removed is used nearby as wall art.

ABOVE: Beyond the tidy grouping of parking court, shed, garage, and residence, a stunning marine vista unfolds all the way to the horizon. OPPOSITE: Over time, encroaching grasses will continue to soften the structure's lower edge.

HIDDEN OVERLOOK

During one of their first visits to a building site in the town of Bourne, Massachusetts, the team from Hutker Architects and the property's owners undertook a small ritual both to honor a home that once stood there and ceremoniously usher in a home soon to rise in the same location. Ensconced on a secluded knob of land poking out into Buzzards Bay, the Cape Cod spot had once belonged to a prominent Boston family whose summer retreat burned down in the 1940s and was never rebuilt. Only a ruinous old foundation was still in evidence, visible as a series of mounds and cavities amid the tangled underbrush. For about half an hour, everyone roamed around collecting bits and pieces of whatever natural or man-made materials caught their eye—stones, wisps of dried grasses, tree bark, metal scraps, chunks of blackened timber that had rested in the earth since the earlier home's fiery demise. A palette of textures and colors began to take shape in the growing pile of finds, a trove of inspiration that would help guide thousands of design choices to come.

The clients were looking to put up a pretty extensive residence—they have a sizable brood of children and grandchildren who all enjoy gathering for holidays and during the summer, so the place needed to gracefully accommodate a crowd. At the same time, they wanted it to embody a casual, farmhouse vibe: free and easy rather than uptight.

Today's completed dwelling is on an undeniably generous scale, spread out from edge to edge of the grounds, yet it seems in no way oppressively grand. Four gabled volumes joined by a flat-roofed connecting spine make up the main house, with a separate fifth gable, enclosing a secondary garage and pool cabana, off to one side. Upper stories sit under the eaves, keeping the overall silhouette low. The owners' requested rustic notes are there, in the vertical siding and rhythmic standing-seam metal roofs, but pared down to a chic modernity. Edges and transitions between one surface and the next are minimally detailed: there are no corner boards, rafter tails, chunky casings, or any of the other kinds of trim you'd expect to see on something calling itself a "farmhouse." Everything about the design breathes clarity and calm.

Colors and materials, too, have been carefully edited, and clearly harken back to that early foraging session on the land: weathered boards the silver-gray of tree bark, copper the reddish brown of an oak leaf clinging to a November branch, and sooty black for the charred *shou sugi ban* paneling applied to the connector structure.

Merely arriving at the house reinforces the sense that you're getting away from the world. It's reached by traversing a wide meadow dotted with strategically scattered birches. From there, a rectangular, shadow-box entry aperture funnels visitors through the front wall before freeing them into a spacious crosswise hallway that gives access to all parts of the building. And water is visible, suddenly, out beyond the twenty-four-foot-tall vaulted ceiling of the great room.

PREVIOUS SPREAD: Seen from downslope by the water, Hidden Overlook might at first be taken for a collection of pleasantly rustic cabins rather than the elegant single residence it actually is. **OPPOSITE:** Visitors to the home are channeled along a boardwalk and through a low shadow-box entry before emerging into the more voluminous spaces indoors.

RIGHT: A broad circulation corridor spans the front of the home. Occasional timbers crossing the ceiling mark important points of transition in the house's structure.
OVERLEAF: In the great room, rugged oak trusses and a board ceiling contrast with the more refined built-in woodwork (which also conceals a television) surrounding the fireplace. At right, ten-foot-tall glass sliders extend the living room out to a terrace that overlooks a picturesque cove.

For, despite the inland experience of its approach, this is a waterfront property. In the back, the pastoral landscape falls off rapidly toward the shore, revealing a harbor view filtered by tall pines and oaks. A mysterious *shou sugi ban* cube stands downslope among the trunks—a bayside art studio that has the feel of a treehouse. On this side of the home, vacation mode hits high gear, and family members can take their pick among a multitude of outdoor-living amenities; decks, terraces, balconies, a screened porch, firepit, pool, and spa are all laid out neatly, ready for use.

Contemporary comfort is also the theme indoors. Although the walls are largely unembellished plaster, painted in a pale lichen hue and with their baseboards and doorframes set flush for simplicity's sake, sensuous oak accents enliven most spaces in the form of beams, planked ceilings, and built-in cabinetry. (A few upstairs "attic" bedrooms sport allover wallpaper, another nod in the direction of cottagey style.) Clean-lined, neutral-toned furnishings wear their sophistication lightly, emphasizing sumptuous finishes instead of elaborate geometries.

Environmental features—not always expected in a house of this sort—include geothermal heating and cooling. Radiant tubing embedded beneath the metal roofing is ample enough to warm the pool and provide domestic hot water. All of the estate's flat-roofed elements—even the little shoreline studio—are planted with suitable greenery. In addition to its thermal advantages, the housetop foliage could also be considered a decorative accent: gaze carefully at the home's facade and you'll notice the fronds and tendrils peeking up here and there. The integration of the home and its surroundings was a major consideration from start to finish. As the flanking meadows and other plantings grow in over time, house and setting will achieve an increasingly synergistic harmony.

This project's success rests on a balancing act, says partner Jim Cappuccino. "There was a nice counterpoint between the rustic associations of some of the materials and forms used, and the very understated detailing of them—and that brings a feeling of modern living to it." The completed residence exudes, in its way, the air of an English country house—reserved from a distance while hinting at openhanded hospitality. Thus, with nods across stylistic boundaries as well as forward and back in time, a venue for family togetherness stands again, after many long decades, in a very special seaside place.

OPPOSITE: A dining table big enough for a crowd occupies the other end of the great room. Cross ties and outsize metal pendant lights help moderate the scale of the lofty ceiling. Off-white walls promote warmth in an otherwise sparely detailed space.

RIGHT: Cooking is an extremely important part of the family's lifestyle, so the kitchen was made with optimal function in mind. Dark-colored drawer fronts were inspired by charred timbers found on the site (leftovers from a house fire in the 1940s), and are balanced by lighter tile and metallic gold accents. Meals are frequently carried out to the screened porch in the background.

ABOVE: The glazed wall in the stairway extends up to the ridgeline of the roof above, letting in a beautiful glow of light through the open stair risers. OPPOSITE: An elegant sitting room for the owners leads to the primary suite. Interior designer Jean Verbridge's decor choices put a premium on richness of both tonality and surface quality.

Just a few dark accents help ground the owners' primarily cream-colored owners' bedroom. The flat ceiling promotes a sense of protection and intimacy, while the beams and boarding still make it special. A small sleeping porch in the center gives out onto a sheltered corner of the landscape.

OPPOSITE: In the primary bath, the dramatic black soaking tub holds court; an outdoor shower (complete with ribbed-stone waterfall) and private garden are accessible behind it. **ABOVE:** A *shou sugi ban*-clad art studio stands among the trees behind the house. **OVERLEAF:** A whole panoply of outdoor living areas, offering different degrees of immersion in the landscape, extends along the dwelling's water side.

BACK RIVER

More often than not, the first question asked about a house's design is "Traditional or contemporary?"—the tacit assumption being that every building will count as either one or the other. (Occasionally a home may be labeled as "transitional," but no one seems to be able to define that term clearly enough to make it useful.) Creatively occupying the fertile borderland between past and present, however, has become a Hutker Architects specialty—to the degree that trying to analyze where traditional leaves off and modern begins in one of the firm's projects risks missing the point entirely. An organic melding of yesterday and today is always there; what's truly important is which specific style notes are struck and the beauty of the harmony they make together. The imaginative evolution of local vernacular is what provides the key.

It was precisely this kind of in-between quality that appealed greatly to one couple in Duxbury, Massachusetts. Both partners had long histories in the vicinity, and they had raised their three college-age sons in a neighborhood close to the town's center that could almost serve as the dictionary definition of classic New England. With the boys now no longer in full-time residence, change beckoned.

So they purchased a property a little farther out from downtown, in a beguilingly romantic district of circuitous lanes where shady woodland leads down to the glowing greens and limitless sky of a coastal salt marsh. Known more for informal summer cottages placed discreetly among the trees than for the grand Colonial mansions that had surrounded the family's previous digs, the area would provide the perfect context for their exploration of a new aesthetic.

Modern or not, they still preferred to make their anticipated home a politely reserved addition to its surroundings. The building therefore nestles into its hillside above the marsh, the main floor at street level. Loose clumps of rhododendron and similar understory growth screen it from the road, making it only sporadically visible—and never all at once—to car and foot traffic passing by. A second story underneath, plus a generous outdoor terrace and pool, are noticeable just from within the property itself—and largely unseen even from down along the shore.

According to Hutker partner Thomas McNeill, an important key to realizing the owners' vision was finding the right mix of historical awareness and fresh thinking. "We did a lot of research, driving around town and taking photographs of nearly every house we thought was authentic and had been there for a hundred years or more," he recalls. "Then we said, 'What speaks to us? What can we pull from these historic examples to inform what the new house can be?'"

Some of the most obvious quotations from Duxbury's architectural heritage reference the John Alden house, a nearby landmark. Two borrowings were structural: an integrated wooden gutter that runs along the roof's edge, charmingly supported by brackets carved out of the rafter tails; and plank-frame windows, which gain an agreeable prominence

PREVIOUS SPREAD: At exactly one point along the street, a momentary view opens straight through the front hedge, into the house, and through to the marsh view beyond.
OPPOSITE: Landscape architect Kris Horiuchi devised the forecourt garden of white-blooming plants as well as the turfed terraces that step down toward the pool.

ABOVE: The integrated wooden rain gutter and its supporting brackets were modeled after those on a local historic home. The entry volume of the house, with its simple horizontal cedar siding, is intentionally reserved in feel. OPPOSITE: Inlaid bronze strips in the floor, along with a change in the direction of the boards, visually continue the flow of the front walkway through to the home's back wall.

ABOVE: The front door opens into the centermost of three metal "aedicules," with smaller doors to a powder room and mudroom at either side. OPPOSITE: A dining area adjoins the living room, demarcated by its own rug and a built-in window seat. OVERLEAF: A pitch-black steel fireplace is the focal point for the light, bright, airy living room. Clerestory windows on all sides make the ceiling appear to levitate. The relaxed furnishings were coordinated by Martha's Vineyard Interior Design.

Pops of darkness—the range hood, wall sconces, and plates and bolts securing the ceiling truss—also add spark to the otherwise all-white kitchen. Windows overlooking the marsh extend down below counter height for a greater range of visibility (and coincidentally allow electrical outlets to be placed out of sight). Suspended industrial-style lights line the edges of the room.

ABOVE: The family's private domain is accessed through this threshold in the kitchen. OPPOSITE: Exterior slats screen light entering the home office as well as providing a handsome backdrop for the open shelving. Strip lighting flush with the plaster ceiling is virtually invisible.

ABOVE LEFT: The stairway acts as a connector between the two halves of the residence, opening to the vertically offset floor levels on each side. **ABOVE RIGHT:** The primary bathroom has its own balcony and outdoor shower. **OPPOSITE:** In the primary bedroom, operable casements flank a central picture window. A small sofa at the foot of the bed faces (of course!) the view.

by extending out from an exterior wall rather than being embedded within it. A third reference to earlier building practices is less specific. Since clapboards, shingles, brick, and white paint are all common currency in the area's visual language, "the initial idea was that maybe we should use clapboards and make part of the house all white," says Mark Hutker. "So we did all these variations using the different materials in different combinations until it felt like the right amount of modern and traditional." By the time the perfect recipe was found, most of the white had disappeared. Only the two chimneys (what are known as "Tory chimneys"—the story being that in pre-Revolutionary America a white chimney with a black cap indicated homeowners who were loyal to the British crown) remain as luminous vertical accents against an otherwise natural wood-tone backdrop.

The "now you see it, now you don't" aspect of the dwelling reaches its peak as a viewer arrives before the property's central entrance. At that point, an angular, boxlike bronze gate embedded in a neatly clipped privet hedge abruptly reveals an arrow-straight axis that transects the landscaped forecourt to pierce both front and back walls of the house and frame a view of the marsh behind. Two more of the bronze threshold structures (Hutker calls them "aedicules," the name deriving from a kind of Roman altar) mark the passage in through the entry door and out again via a pristine picture window in the rear. The effect is somehow ceremonial, even archaic and monumental in its way, reminiscent of a metallic Stonehenge or Babylon's Ishtar Gate.

The residence lives larger than it looks, with social spaces and family bedroom suites (and a private office) broken out in two separate gabled volumes coupled by a "hyphen" enclosing the home's main stair. There's a horizontal division of functions, too, with parents ensconced on the upper floors and the younger generation's territory mostly on the lower, walkout level, ready for whenever they choose to visit. The need to pack a maximum of function into a restricted footprint gave rise as well to one of the home's most dramatic features: a screened porch that cantilevers out a full sixteen feet over the pool terrace, thus layering two distinct outdoor living experiences on top of the area ordinarily required for one.

Evoking memories of what has come before while also achieving something new and different, the house has been very well received by the community. As a response to its owners' intentions, McNeill says, it hit the mark spot-on. "It perfectly suits who they are and how they live in the town. It's like a reflection of them in the best possible way."

OPPOSITE: A typical Hutker "hyphen" links two larger architectural volumes. The home's rear is largely transparent for maximum engagement with nature.
OVERLEAF: Although sheltered from the street for privacy, Back River's screened porch, terrace, and pool are gloriously open to the neighboring coastal salt marsh.

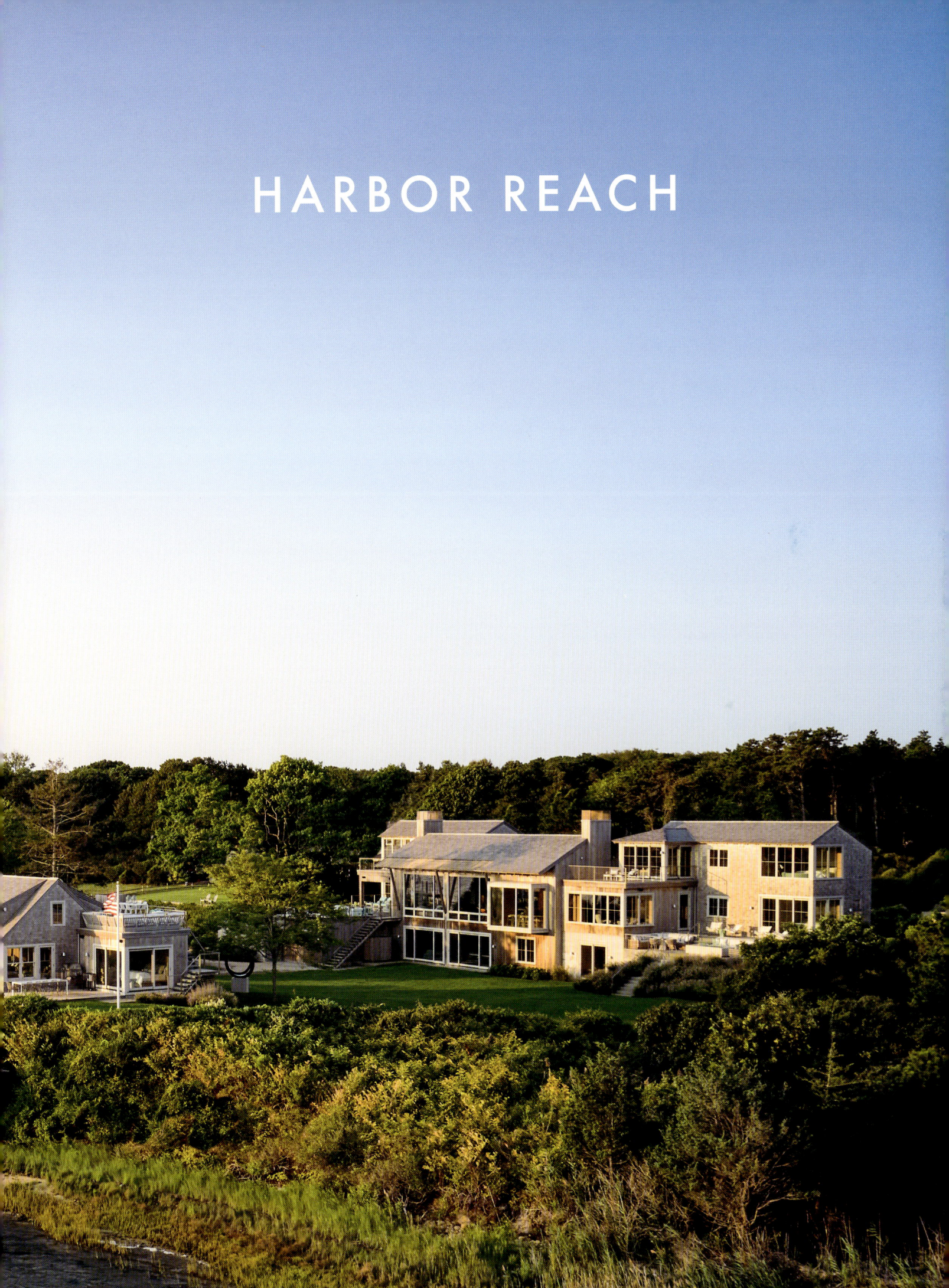

HARBOR REACH

PREVIOUS SPREAD: The paired structures of Harbor Reach—one large, one smaller—look out toward Chappaquiddick Island. ABOVE: An entry garden on the landward side makes for a pleasant journey to the front door. OPPOSITE: The stairway in one of the home's two residential volumes jogs around a corner. The pole-mounted chandelier is a perfect accent, glowing in the wraparound window at night.

For someone boating in from Katama Bay toward the harbor, this little building wouldn't draw much attention. At first glance it's simply an unassuming local cottage perched waterside along the passage between Chappaquiddick and the main island of Martha's Vineyard: shed dormers, exposed rafter tails, shingles, white trim—the usual features of archetypal New England. Recently renovated, perhaps, but nothing too flashy.

Only when the eye pulls back to take in the much broader architectural panorama spread out behind the modest shoreline structure does it become clear that something truly special is going on. The small house straddling the bluff, its feet planted firmly in the past, is only one of a pair of buildings that make up this quietly spectacular residence. Its grander partner, hugging the far edge of the property, extends laterally from one end of the site to the other, a considerably more contemporary mosaic of weathering wood, glass, and board-formed concrete. The two buildings stand in balanced opposition, facing each other across an immaculate stretch of lawn that in the summer months is an almost constant site for gathering and impromptu games of soccer and lacrosse.

Visitors arriving on the landward side of the home experience a different, equally compelling, narrative of approach. A quiet dirt lane opens unexpectedly onto a long, narrow garden packed with hydrangeas and tasseled grasses. To the right, two-story shingled wings flank a low pavilion clad in vertical cedar boards, whose front door is itself centered between generously scaled banks of windows that look out to the hidden inland oasis of foliage.

Step in through the front door, however, and immediately beyond the flat-ceilinged entry your view will suddenly be drawn up and up. You've reached the core of the home, what Mark Hutker terms the "life room: because that's where we share life and make memories." A combined living-dining-entertaining space, the life room sits beneath a lofty, asymmetrical saltbox roof, higher on the far side where it caps broad expanses of glass framing a choice vista of land and water—with the little bluff house in the foreground—and, importantly, sky. "Oftentimes we underestimate the sky view, because we're so focused on the water," says Hutker partner Jim Cappuccino. "The shape of this roof begins to lift that perspective; it elevates your senses."

Running along the landward side of the main house is a broad interior corridor that joins the two taller wings, each of which encloses a pair of bedroom suites. The segregated arrangement allows the homeowners (plus their children and guests) to enjoy privacy when they want it, and togetherness when they're in a social mood. A liberal scattering of terraces and decks in assorted shapes and sizes ensures that sun and fresh air are always within easy reach.

The bluff cottage, meanwhile, is intended for pure enjoyment. Like its exterior, the interior appears entirely traditional, even a bit rustic—with rafters and wall studs exposed as if a vintage structure had simply been gutted and painted white (instead of being entirely rebuilt, as actually happened). The family members are avid entertainers (especially well known, locally, for their annual 1970s-themed disco affair), and they refer to this as their "party barn."

ABOVE: An assortment of setbacks, bump-outs, awning overhangs, and other architectural features animates the water-facing facade of the main home. Twin chimneys brace the ends of the central pavilion, while bedroom wings extend on both sides. A lower level, giving out onto the lawn, houses mostly recreational spaces.

The dining area in the "life room" almost has the feel of a cocktail lounge. Boston-based interior designer Heather Wells chose powdery colors for the furniture to complement, but not upstage, bright-hued artworks collected by the owners specifically for this house.

Subdued cabinetry and countertops in the kitchen let the highly figured stone backsplash really shine. Panels set into it slide aside to reveal shelving for spices and oils. A thick oak threshold at right leads to the family room.

Architect Jim Cappuccino conceived the system of stainless-steel posts and tie rods that lends visible structure to the asymmetrical ceiling. The composition of the stone-faced fireplace wall, contemporary as it looks, is governed by the ancient proportions of the Golden Section.

ABOVE: A roof walk connecting the two bedroom pavilions mirrors the course of an interior passageway on the ground floor.
OPPOSITE: Seen from below, the zigzags of the oak ribbon stair generate a marvelous pattern of light and shadow.

In its new guise, the one-and-a-half-story ceiling has become an interior firmament, spangled with blue and white glass globes like a galaxy of stars (or bubbles, maybe), and it anchors a suspended sleeping loft whose mirrored underside serves as a ceiling for the kitchen. (An additional fun touch: the loft is accessed via a secret stairway concealed in what looks like a pantry cabinet.) Airy, bright, and set almost on top of the water, it's hard to imagine a more apt site for revelry.

As part of its transformation, the cottage also acquired a 500-square-foot modern extension housing what will eventually (once the kids are grown) become the owners' primary bed and bath suite. Resting on the flat roof above is perhaps the jewel of the property: the so-called Osprey Nest, a super-cozy deck, complete with wraparound banquettes and a gas firepit, that looks along the shore toward the busy inner harbor, where white boats dot the surface like sugar grains spilled across a tabletop.

These paired structures—the main house and the bluff cottage—are the twin poles around which family life revolves, two centers of gravity bordering the central lawn.

"Early on we were talking about this project having all the amenities of a boutique inn," says Cappuccino. And so it does. At a deeper level, though, the residence is an exercise in equilibrium. First is "how the life room pavilion looks in both directions," Hutker observes. "The great view is on the water side, but that beautiful landscape we created is on the opposite side and it balances the house in a nice way." Then there is the manner in which the two buildings jointly occupy the site: pushing the larger one back to the property's inland edge "makes this middle space, this active lawn, as gracious as it could be, and, as you can see, it allows the architecture to breathe."

Grand, yet not at all overpowering, main house and bluff house coexist in a mix that feels definitely of the moment while at the same time melding harmoniously into the community's historic architectural setting. And really, the story of finding an appropriate balance is one that could apply to almost all Hutker projects. Combining the right proportions of heart and mind, aesthetics and utility, luxury and restraint, is what the firm has long been known for, and the same ideals continue to guide the architects' thinking today.

OPPOSITE: Whitewashed planks add subtle texture to the ceiling of the owners' upstairs sitting room. A Sputnik-style chandelier furthers the home's overall midcentury vibe. A twin to the blue glass railing at right encloses the pool outside.

ABOVE: Hutker bedrooms typically offer more than one kind of living experience. Here, the bed is tucked securely between opaque walls for restful sleep, while the facing sofa is immersed in a wraparound view toward the harbor.
OPPOSITE: In one of the guest baths, the mirror is suspended in front of a window. OVERLEAF: The pool and an assortment of terraces and balconies are oriented toward the shoreline "party barn" cottage and the water.

ABOVE: A bedroom inside the shoreline cottage—and its attached roof deck—will one day be taken over by the homeowners.
OPPOSITE: The cottage is a re-creation of an earlier structure whose second floor was removed. The resulting double-height entertaining space includes a full kitchen and an open sleeping loft that is secretly accessed through the cabinetry on the right.
OVERLEAF: A porch and deck next to the infinity-edge pool are perfect locations for enjoying a cocktail and watching the boats go by.

ABOUT THE FIRM

For more than thirty-five years, Hutker Architects has been collaborating with families and individuals to create one-of-a-kind homes that are uniquely suited to the particulars of their location and the life patterns of the people who occupy them.

Having designed more than three hundred houses along the New England shore and beyond, we are committed to the principle of "build once, well." We believe in the importance of superior craftsmanship born from an inquiry into the historic architecture and narrative of each project's location, which becomes a wellspring of inspiration for original, evolutionary new work.

Today, Hutker Architects is a team of seventy professionals who share the belief that houses represent the "social atom," the essential definer of family and cultural heritage. Our team is passionate about the power of meaningful architecture and committed to harnessing our individual talents toward a common goal: advancing the art of dwelling.

We are continually inspired by the challenge of making places that feel like "home" to each client. Whether designing a primary dwelling or a seasonal retreat, we strive to produce inviting, adaptable houses that are well suited for today and will continue to be enjoyed for generations.

Building on our experience, and through further research and design, our vision is to create a new standard for custom homes to be both passive in their demands on their environment and community and active in their influence on the well-being of their inhabitants.

Combining the right proportions of heart and mind, aesthetics and utility, luxury and restraint, is what the firm has long been known for—and the same ideals will continue to guide Hutker Architects into the future.

FALMOUTH
BACK FROM LEFT: Liam Johnson, Aaron Teves, Nicole Mant, Julie Bangert, John DiSalvo, Kevin Schreur

MIDDLE FROM LEFT: Ally Stecich, Ally Hess, Casey Clarke, Danielle Raciti, Jaifer Sultan, Cory Pereira, Mark Hutker, Mary Rogers, Jim Cappuccino, Bernadette Robinson, Carol Ann Livingstone, Matt Schiffer, Erin Levin

FRONT FROM LEFT: Charles e. Orr, Ghillie, Stacey Sarber, Nancy Swensson, Nancy Peters

MARTHA'S VINEYARD
BACK LEFT TO RIGHT: Tom Shockey, Kelly O'Hara, Christian Donato, Karen Chesney, Sarah Ives, Weston Halkyard, Phil Regan, Eric Dori

FRONT LEFT TO RIGHT: Nicole Edmonds, Addy, Audrey Snare, Greg Ehrman, Rob Aryee, Brittany Knowlton, Sean Dougherty, Matthew Cramer

PLYMOUTH
BACK LEFT TO RIGHT: Thomas McNeill, Oliver Orwig, Casey Clarke, Jessica Kelly, Jonathan Fox

FRONT LEFT TO RIGHT: John Kim, Vivian Scherer, Marissa Wolinsky, Megan Jewell, Anthony Kho Sasih, Laura Brooks

BOSTON
BACK LEFT TO RIGHT: Tony Bene, Michael Black, Zach Fields, Jim Cappuccino

FRONT LEFT TO RIGHT: Mark Hutker, Amy Rogers, Acadia Alden, Deepa Parthasarathy, Ryan Alcaidinho

NOT PICTURED:
Emily Avakian, Whitney Bickford, Susie Himel, Megan Langlois, Jake Lefeber, Diana Lin, Olivia Martin, Scott McCullough, Morgan Miller, Graham Parks, Eder Romero, Sarah Soltes, Greg Whiting

PROJECT CREDITS

THREE GABLES, page 14
Partner: Mark Hutker, FAIA
Principal: Matthew Schiffer, AIA
Project Manager: Ryan Alcaidinho
Project Team: Kevin Schreur
Interior Design: Thom Filicia, Inc.
Builder: Hobbs, Inc.

BREEZY POINT, page 36
Partner: Phil Regan
Project Manager: Tom Shockey
Project Team: Rob Aryee, Morgan Miller, Paul Commito
Interior Design: Hutker Architects
Landscape Architect: Horiuchi Solien, Inc.
Builder: J. G. Early Contractor and Builder, Inc.

BREACHING ROCK, page 54
Partner: Gregory Ehrman, AIA
Project Manager: Sean Dougherty, LEED AP
Project Team: Sarah Ives, Weston Halkyard, Jake Lefeber
Landscape Architect: Horiuchi Solien, Inc
Garden Design: Multiflora
Builder: Mark Hurwitz Designer Builder

THE GRANGE, page 110
Partner: Gregory Ehrman, AIA
Project Manager: Scott McCullough, AIA
Project Team: Audrey Snare, Aaron Teves, Morgan Miller
Interior Design: Homeowner
Landscape Architect: Wagner Hodgson Landscape Architecture
Builder: Sisler Builders, Inc.

FEN'S EDGE, page 128
Partner: Thomas McNeill, AIA, Mark Hutker, FAIA
Project Manager: Jonathan Fox, AIA
Project Team: Laura Brooks, AIA, Anthony Kho Sasih
Interior Design: Studio Frank
Landscape Architect: Katherine Field and Associates, Inc.
Builder: Evergreen Building Systems

BIG BLUFF, page 146
Partner: Mark Hutker, FAIA
Principal: Matthew Cramer, AIA
Project Team: Sean Dougherty, LEED AP, Rob Aryee
Interior Design: Hutker Architects
Landscape Architect:t: Dan Gordon Landscape Architects
Builder: J. G. Early Contractor and Builder, Inc.

GREAT POND, page 186
Partner: Gregory Ehrman, AIA
Project Manager: Sean Dougherty, LEED AP
Project Team: Stacey Sarber
Interior Design: Hutker Architects
Landscape Architect: Lil Province
Builder: Adam T., Inc.

HIDDEN OVERLOOK, page 202
Partner: Jim Cappuccino, AIA
Project Manager: Deepa Parthasarathy
Project Team: Erin Levin
Interior Design: SV Design, Architecture + Interiors
Landscape Architect: Horiuchi Solien, Inc.
Builder: Payne Bouchier Fine Home Builders

BACK RIVER, page 222
Partner: Thomas McNeill, AIA, Mark Hutker, FAIA
Project Manager: Deepa Parthasarathy
Interior Design: Martha's Vineyard Interior Design
Landscape Architect: Horiuchi Solien, Inc.
Builder: Sea View Construction

ISLAND AERIE, page 78
Partner: Gregory Ehrman, AIA
Project Manager: Scott McCullough, AIA
Project Team: Stacey Sarber, Weston Halkyard
Interior Design: Lauren Liess Interiors
Landscape Architect: Campion Hruby Landscape Architects
Builder: The Banks Development Co. Custom Home Builders

SUNSET HILL, page 94
Partner: Phil Regan
Project Manager: Tom Shockey
Project Team: Stacey Sarber, Olivia Martin
Interior Design: Hutker Architects
Landscape Architect: Horiuchi Solien, Inc.
Builder: Martha's Vineyard Construction Company

LEDGE HOUSE, page 164
Partner: Thomas McNeill, AIA, Mark Hutker, FAIA
Project Manager: Ryan Alcaidinho
Interior Design: Hutker Architects
Landscape Architect: Gregory Lombardi Design
Builder: Cum Laude Group, Inc.

HARBOR REACH, page 242
Partner: Mark Hutker, FAIA, Jim Cappuccino, AIA
Project Manager: Mackenzie Pratt, AIA
Project Team: Erin Levin, Deepa Parthasarathy, Michael Black
Interior Design: Heather Wells, Inc.
Landscape Architect: Horiuchi Solien, Inc.
Builder: Rosbeck Builders

ADDITIONAL COLLABORATORS:

Against the Grain Cabinetmakers, Architectural Timber & Millwork, Inc., Artisan Engineering, Barney Zeitz, Bay Engineering, Inc., Belisle Architectural Windows and Doors, Billy Hoff, BluBlk, Cape Cod Passive House, Cataumet Sawmill, Connecticut Stone, Duratherm Window Company, Dynamic Fenestration, Grenier Engineering, PC, Hanschka Fine Metalwork, Herrick and White Architectural Woodworkers, Hope's Windows, Inc., John Thayer Cabinetmakers, JSR Adaptive Energy Solutions, LLC, Landscope, Inc., Loewen Windows, LS Group, MAKE, Makrowin, Marshall Farm Wood-Works, Maverick Integration, Multiflora, MV Color & Finish, Inc., Orsman Design, Paradis MetalWorks, Plain English Design, R. P. Marzilli Landscape Professionals, Reilly Architectural, Siegel Structural Engineers, Stephen Stimson Associates Landscape Architects, Inc., Stone Soup Concrete, Inc., System 7 Technology Design, TE2 Engineering, The Hudson Company, Thread Workroom, Venegas and Company, Vintage & Specialty Wood, Whetstone Workshop

ACKNOWLEDGMENTS

It was a true pleasure bringing together individuals and teams with incredible knowledge, talent, and creativity to collaborate on this book. Literally hundreds of people contributed in some way to the making of the houses featured in these pages; I have the space to call out only a few of them in particular here, but am profoundly grateful to everyone who was involved.

The book's introduction outlines how our work is inspired by client stories; thus, these acknowledgments must begin with thanking those clients—our patrons—for the trust they bestow on us at Hutker Architects. We feel it is an act of stewardship to assume responsibility for creating homes that resonate with each family and each community in which a dwelling is made. The relationships that are born with every project are dear to us, and watching families thrive in their finished homes gives us the deepest satisfaction.

Next, I want to celebrate my HA colleagues, whose skills, conviction, inventiveness, and hard work unite to make possible the uplifting environments we bring into being as a firm. All counted, the firm's partners, Jim Cappuccino, Greg Ehrman, Tom McNeill, Charles Orr, and Phil Regan; principals Ryan Alcaidinho, Julie Bangert, Matt Cramer, Sean Dougherty, and Matt Schiffer; and CEO Mary Rogers represent more than 237 years of shared work history—that's definitely worth acknowledging! Every day, we are blessed with the opportunity of doing together something that we love with great passion and commitment. The authentic friendships that have evolved are indelible.

Since our last book came out, Hutker Architects' staff has grown twofold and we've opened two additional offices. Our interiors group is emerging as an important element of the firm, devising personalized and expressive spaces that beautifully complement our architecture. On par with HA's design acumen, our business and administrative personnel must be recognized for underpinning our enterprise with the requisite structure that allows us to focus on plans and clients. And to the balance of our HA team, each so critical to our combined success, I extend my most genuine appreciation for all you do.

Nancy Swensson, my invaluable special assistant on the book and in general, is an endlessly patient and good-humored facilitator of our work. Photo shoots and styling were ably arranged by Julie Bangert, Danielle Raciti, and Ally Stecich.

I owe an incalculable debt to all of these people not just for their artistic contributions to this book but for their enthusiasm and dedication to our firm throughout the years.

Beautiful photography is, of course, essential for conveying the experience of architecture in published form. We were fortunate to have Michael

J. Lee's discerning eye to help capture many of the homes in this book. David Burroughs, Phillip Ennis, Marc Fairstein, Nick Johnson, Neil Landino, Joshua McHugh, Helen Norman, Kate Rogan, and David Welch also supplied key images.

Kyle Hoepner, who cowrote the text, has been a friend for decades. I credit him and Kathy Bush-Dutton, the publisher of *New England Home* magazine, for bringing the residential design community together through the New England Design Hall of Fame and 5 Under 40 awards programs. Kyle is one of the most perceptive observers of architecture in our region, and he has the insight to put our work in context. He is a strong, emotive writer and has captured the narrative of each home with acuity and grace.

Equally vital are the people behind the making of the book itself. Superlative agents and book packagers Jill Cohen and Melissa Powell led the way with an early pitch to Monacelli and their unfailingly useful advice, as well as assembling the production crew that includes graphic designers Doug Turshen and David Huang. Special thanks are due to Monacelli publisher Philip Ruppel, along with editors Jenny Florence and Sean Newcott, for their informed and expert guidance. I'm indebted to all of these people for recognizing meaning in our work and making the publication process an enriching experience. Each of them is an extraordinary professional; their candor and counsel helped us see our work from a different perspective and curate these examples from our oeuvre.

Hutker Architects' many consultants and collaborators in the field—interior designers, landscape architects, builders, engineers, makers, and artists—are apex professionals. We learn from one another in manifold ways, which ensures that growth is always in the future. I thank them all for further connecting our homes to place with their collective knowledge, aesthetic gifts, and personalities. How a house is made is important to making it better.

Cheers to the significant others and families who nurture our teammates. Residential design is a "passion sport," and it is often difficult to get a project out of your mind once you've immersed yourself in it. The willingness of friends and loved ones to put up with our demanding schedules is an indispensable asset.

Finally, I'd like to thank my family. My wife, Carla, who has been my personal foundation and most sensitive critic through all the years leading up to and beyond our ruby anniversary, is Hutker Architects' most adored ambassador. Evan, Ana, Harly, Emma, and Owen uplift me with their love and zest. And ongoing deep gratitude to all my friends for their kindness, understanding, and encouragement.

—Mark A. Hutker, FAIA